BORDER

Books by Peter Bennet

First Impressions, with Rosemary Scott and Dave Stagg (Mandeville Press, 1983)

Sky-Riding (Peterloo Poets, 1984)

The Border Hunt (Jackson's Arm, 1986)

A Clee Sequence (Lincolnshire and Humberside Arts, 1986)

All the Real (Flambard Press, 1994)

The Long Pack (Flambard Press, 2002)

Ha-Ha (Smith/Doorstop, 2003)

Noctua (Shoestring Press, 2004)

Goblin Lawn: New & Selected Poems (Flambard Press, 2005)

The Glass Swarm (Flambard Press, 2008)

Bobby Bendick's Ride, with drawings by Birtley Aris (Enchiridion, 2010)

The Game of Bear (Flambard Press, 2011)

Border (Bloodaxe Books, 2013)

PETER BENNET

BORDER

BLOODAXE BOOKS

ISBN: 978 1 85224 993 9

First published 2013 by
Bloodaxe Books Ltd,
Highgreen,
Tarset,
Northumberland NE48 1RP.

www.bloodaxebooks.com
For further information about Bloodaxe titles
please visit our website or write to
the above address for a catalogue.

Cover design: Neil Astley & Pamela Robertson-Pearce.

Printed in Great Britain by Bell & Bain Limited, Glasgow, Scotland, on
acid-free paper sourced from mills with FSC chain of custody certification.

For Peter and Margaret Lewis

ACKNOWLEDGEMENTS

The first three sections of this edition comprise poems reprinted from these books: *Goblin Lawn: New and Selected Poems* (2005), *The Glass Swarm* (2008) and *The Game of Bear* (2011), all published by Flambard Press. Thanks are also due to Five Leaves Publications, Indigo Dreams Publishing, Iron Press, Other Poetry Editions, Shoestring Press and Smith/ Doorstop Books.

Poems have appeared in the anthologies *North by North East,* the region's contemporary poetry; *Speaking English,* a festschrift for John Lucas; *Still Standen*, a festschrift for Michael Standen; *In Your Own Time*, the Northern Poetry Workshop anthology; and *A Speaking Silence: Quaker poets of today*. I am grateful to the editors: R.V. Bailey, James Roderick Burns, Andy Croft, Cynthia Fuller, Stevie Krayer and Gerry Wardle. Poems have also appeared in *The Rialto, The Poetry Salzburg Review, The Times Literary Supplement, The Poetry Book Society Bulletin* and *The Guardian.*

'The Redesdale Rowan' was commissioned by Culture North East for the Sense of Place project and 'Snow at Fourlawshill Top' was commisioned by New Writing North and Arts Council England. I am indebted to New Writing North for Time to Write awards and to Arts Council England for financial help to travel to France, Austria and South Africa in pursuit of Dornford Yates.

CONTENTS

from **GOBLIN LAWN** (2005)

12 Ha-Ha
13 Genealogy
14 Content
15 Filming the Life
16 Spalpeen
17 Cha-Cha-Cha
19 Nothing Worse
20 Tithonus at Kielder
21 THE LONG PACK
41 The Border
42 Fairytale
43 Inyuyucoy
44 Woodsmoke
45 The Little Flame
46 The Punt *Nixie*
47 Uncle George and the Snow Bunting
49 The Fossil
50 The Damp Harmonium
51 The Pigeon Loft
52 The Sisters
53 Squiffy
54 Breathe Carefully
55 The Intervention
56 Ogress
57 Listening Duty
58 The Banner Men
60 The Imp
61 The Cypher
62 The Sally Garden
63 The Angel
64 Miss Daphne
65 JIGGER NODS

from **THE GLASS SWARM** (2008)

89 Sir Entrepreneur
90 The Naturalist
91 The Silver of the Mirror
93 The Squirrel
94 Quince Blossom
95 The Pickle Tub
96 Danse Macabre
98 Cuneiform
99 The Redesdale Rowan
100 The Lens
101 The Parting
102 Sea Fever
103 The Tourist
104 Après-midi
105 St George's Day
106 Black Country Browning
107 FOLLY WOOD
119 The Brass Band
121 The Cockatrice
122 The Acorn
123 The Green Corn
124 Recessional
125 The Ballroom at Blaxter Hall
126 The Stitchers
127 Home is the Sailor
128 Greta
130 The Ventriloquist and the Wooden Girl
131 Wentletraps
133 The Bather
134 Snow at Fourlawshill Top

from **THE GAME OF BEAR** (2011)

136 The Tower
137 The Empress
138 Gustav Mahler Returns to Maiernigg

139 Unity in the Englischer Garten
140 The Claxon Case
142 Fortitude
143 The Devil
144 The Juggler
145 The Good Child
146 Penny Dreadful
147 BOBBY BENDICK'S RIDE
156 *Artemis Before a Prospect of Blaxter Hall*
157 The Vacant Blue
158 The Night Chapel
159 Epithalamium
160 A Shepherd to His Lass
161 The Fool
162 Le Pendu
163 Sentinels
164 The Drowned Heads
165 The Owl Herb
166 Spraunce
168 The Graiae and the Matelot
169 The Star
170 The Chrysalis
171 An Evening on the River
172 A Slice of Lime

NEW POEMS (2013)

175 The African Queen
176 The Square
177 Vampire Writers
178 Augenlicht
179 Comb Hill
180 Future Perfect
181 Mademoiselle de Silhouette
182 Uncle Benson
184 Curiosity in Bolam Woods
185 Venus Among the Ruins

186 The Mistress
187 The Podiatrists
188 The Suitor
189 Eden Lodge
190 The Fancier
191 Summer on Fourlaws Fell

193 NOTES

FROM

Goblin Lawn

(2005)

Ha-Ha

Let me affirm that what I have not done
remains a plant so valueless
that I have never learned its shape or name.

It thrives, a clump of uncommitted spirit,
between me and the *saut-de-loup*, or *ha-ha.*

It was in Paris, or on the Riviera,
entre deux guerres, for sure, that someone
quite unknown to me, but close,
had picked a bunch, and tied it with a ribbon,
to throw into a grave I will not enter.

Genealogy

Since yesterday, it seems, the maps have changed,
the church clock cannot tell the time,
the names you want have faded from the microfiche,
and from the xeroxed parish registers.

The village is beneath the town,
the town is underneath the city.

Just think, the letter from your ancestor
that would have made the whole thing clear, the task
so simple, put aside and never finished,
because a moth got in the inkwell.

Call it a day.

You'd starve, in any case, if you went back,
the past contains no sustenance,
the birthday cakes are grey with dust,
the orchards there grow only apple cores.

Look now, at the changing creature
here in the hedge, made out of leaves: its tiny
limbs reach out for recognition.

Its colour goes so suddenly from green
to splintering silver: can you see it, dare you touch?

Content

Time ripens in abundance, hanging
unplucked while he examines the horizon,
or shies selected stones at driftwood.

Since exile here, he understands
he is a figment of his own imagination.

His mind is now becoming like the ocean
on which he sometimes fancies glimpses
of distant ships, or makes some speck
a swimmer's head, small waves
the rocking angles of a swimmer's arms.

Solitude, and lack of tools or toys
do not constrain him: he can visit
all his wishes, walk or run, repeat his journeys,
act on impulses or cancel them,
and name things or decide to leave them nameless.

He is content to be passed over
by infrequent clouds, and birds
with gaudy wings and human voices.

He disregards the long-haul airliner
whose dreamy passengers can hardly see
his island, let alone
the threats to trespassers he has inscribed
in foliage across the broadest beach.

Filming the Life

Your sisters have agreed to drag their skirts
across the fields where trees are shrugging
coldly, as it is October,
towards the lane with hedges, and the gate
where gravel leads to wider gravel,
and damp-stains on the quoining of the manse.

We have the Bible on the hallstand,
adjacent to the wet umbrella,
and cabbage in a kitchen full of women.

The draughts at ankle-height across the flagstones
come from the hills on which your father wanders,
prising sermons from the mist and boulders.

Your role now is to find an upstairs room,
and be the ghost-child at a pointed window,
offering his breath to glass
in order to inscribe it, and then seeing
a darker world on which his name is weeping.

You are too sickly to grow old,
and will not live to see your pamphlets smoulder
in every bookshop of the revolution.

Spalpeen

Time's up for you inside my myth,
so shout at every turning of the tune,
and clap your hands
to have this moment for your pleasure.

Fact steps forward to reveal you,
clean-shaven, and of medium height,
like every spalpeen in the land.

Outside, trams flash and clang
through Celtic twilight, and the rain
that slicks the courtyard of the School of Art
shines the stone limbs of Cuchulain,
the lord of skirmish and unlucky frolic.

You gave me nothing but permission.

I was your shadow, and my dumb attention
a story harped on long ago
which made for grief, just as the love
of my fair rival, Kathleen of the duffel coat,
led towards the lake of weeping.

Cha-Cha-Cha

Evening achieves a winter definition:
the gravel stark between metallic laurels,
and your french window lit too brightly
to countenance my pale reflection.

I formed you out of fog and petrol fumes
outside the walls of colleges
where gargoyles sneer above shut doors,
and now I'm here, according to my custom,
to tap discreetly on your glass and enter
for sherry, and rich conversation
among your art and incunabula.

Although your back is turned towards me,
I see your well-trimmed head is as I shaped it,
together with the light, informal jacket
above dark trousers with an iron crease.

There should not be a gramophone, however,
unless for Mozart, and it puzzles me
to hear one faintly honking cha-cha-cha.

You are my creature and my ideal tutor,
the man to help me get my thinking baked
and spiced with wit and erudition,
the chum I can rely on always
urbanely to correct my sentences.

But please remember that your cosy room
will freeze if ever I should wish it,
and you will shrivel and no longer be.

Forgive me if I seem at all ungrateful.

It's who you're talking to that makes me peevish,
her sleek legs angled to the hearth
from that deep armchair sacred to philosophy,
and how, when she in turn begins to speak,
her head uptilts, a smoke-ring hanging,
to notice me, then mock me with a wink.

Nothing Worse

You do not know this, but your standard lamp
has been sawn through, a foot below the shade.

Meanwhile, the river swells and flows on grass,
a pasture swallowing its fences, green
contending, overcoming green, until
the stink and rush, from this high viaduct,
suggests that nothing human will outlast
leeching eels, and rain, and livid sky.

Come back with me into your sitting room.

The party you walked out on has concluded
in nothing worse than friendly sabotage.

Tithonus at Kielder

Since death avoids you, every longed-for morning
hurts worse than death, and evenings turn
from grey to purple without hope.

Cheer up, old grasshopper, at least
you had the guts to claim the dawn
before the hours indignant worked their wills.

The woods decay and fall, so fell
and plant again, and celebrate your days
as if they danced like sunlit leaves
caught in the backstream of a timber waggon
returning on its silver wheels.

THE LONG PACK

I tremble to tell you! We are all gone,
for it is a living pack.

JAMES HOGG

Northumberland is a rough county.

SIR NIKOLAUS PEVSNER

I

Darkness is my second mother,
the pack a double blindness, in whose caul
I must not move,
but grip my butcher's knife, my silver whistle,
and wait till silence matches dark,
to cut free like a savage child.

I am about my act, my strange acte,
my worke, my strange work.

II

Now Bellingham is briefly hers.

The oiled gate
is quiet as a book to open.

Inside, the yew tree is a flame's
dark opposite,
smudged upon the inner eye,
it struggles upward, angled to its stem,
and cannot leave the ground.

My stone's a lid on grass,
but mind is calling me to mind, as if
I might be here awake and answering
bones above the layered bones.

The iron latch-tail chills,
and clings to moisture on her palm.

I'm seeing what I don't remember,
and so are you, imagining my fear,
and sacking chafing at my face.

I breathe stale merchandise,
and, as a lantern flares through cloth,
embrace a tremor in the air.

Whosoever hears of it,
both his ears shall tingle.

III

At sunset, Midas fished the Tyne,
or else the gentry of Northumberland
are melting all their riches down.

Gold slides past kingcups to the sea,
but here, where common boulders sit,
colours are of coal and lead.

My father stumbles from the flow:
his hands are empty, but his head
has feasted on philosophy.

That man he countless times heard preach
against the rule and stink of priests maintained,
one Lord's day sixty years ago,
he met God walking in an open field,
to his eyes seeming strange,
a man deformed, clad in patched clouts.

God looked wishly on him, and he pittied God.

The Tyne would bubble like a sore
if it absorbed
the rage my father steeps in it.

Our supper slips to deeper water.

IV

Time rattles in the ewe's throat.

Mist blots up stories from the fell,
muffles moorland industry, conceals
herd and soldier, park and steading,
tumulus and battlestone,
the horse that bolted with the bride,
lots drawn, stratagems forgotten.

The dead do not know who they are
until they are remembered.

V

A fly strums glass,
and bumps the distances your window holds.

Blue hills, remembering to be
Roxburghshire, across the Border,
stand for all that's torn away,
like Houxty Wood:
the nymphs lamenting for their dear resort.

The fly is stitching
shreds of history to hills,
and patching nearer times with fields.

The past lies in the sun beyond the pane.

Art poor? Yea, very poor, said He.

VI

At Warden, where the two Tynes meet
behind my father's empty hands,
I see the solemn water break
into a curve of countless brilliants
across my memory, as rich and starry
as Colonel Ridley's chandeliers,
and one great salmon in their midst
stand upon its tail for ever.

This is a true story, most true in the history.

The fish is one of diverse signs
that comfort me
in this concealment where I am
still visible,
if you will please imagine it.

The plague of God is in your purses,
did you not see my hand stretched out?

VII

She thumbs an apple in her pocket
and somewhere thunder scrapes a drum.

The fieldgate jigs,
its wreckage flouncing baler-twine.

Sunlight on a shattered gable
hints at past prosperity:
The Orchard on its tidy portion.

Drystone dikes beside the path
rise again among the nettles,
and deeply fumbling ruts reveal

the old highroad across the Rede,
broad enough for carts to pass, or haul
harvest towers, two abreast.

Tyme tryeth Troth.

Her apple pleases
a roan mare by the broken barn.

VIII

The Jacobite rose-bush
strikes your wall with small, white blossoms.

Fallen petals sign the ground:
Derwentwater, Forster, Mad Jack Hall.

Northumberland is Arcady.

The paperback you've pushed aside
has Radcliffe an Initiate,
the rose a mystery
bred by the Prieuré de Sion.

IX

It is meat and drink to an Angel
to swear a full-mouthed oath.

The deeds and discourse
of that great engine of disorder, Richard Last,
so pressed my father's waxy spirit
that two-score years of witnessing
and sundry buffetings we all and each endured
have not ground smooth their stamp.

Neither the death of Mr Last
in this world, or the dissolution
of his lewd company,
nor yet the ruination of our farm,
the self-same Orchard, could abate
his whistling multifarious fancies.

My deer ones consider,
here is no lodging, no safe habitation.

X

Lord of the wood was my game once:
Rob o' Risingham and Robin Hood,
the king within the oak in summer time.

The Oak-Leaves me embroyder all,
between them Caterpillars crawl
and Ivy, with familiar trails,
me licks, and clasps, and curls, and hales.

A boy's face, smiling among leaves,
tells me I shall live again.

XI

To be alone is always new.

Outside your window, past the rosebush
and the garden, moorland pasture
steeps its skirts in the arriving night.

Booze turns the landscape into art.

Cloudscapes you have watched since noon
are smouldering and charged with thunder,

while fells regroup as gloomy leas
and boskage: school of Claude Lorraine.

Pools and streams snag threads of light
in jagged valleys and defiles.

Above Greenrigg, a crabwise track
climbs gothic heights
towards a crumbling tower of cumulus.

You see a well, which sad trees overhang,
and flame and woodsmoke by a ruined arch,
or in some bouldered clearing,
and, always there, the same two countrymen
in ragged costume of their age.

The elder stoops to coax the fire, the younger
leans forward on his staff. Sometimes
they picturesquely fish a stream
or crouch as if in hope beside the path.

I am found of those that sought me not.

XII

The Karrimor rucksack biffs the ground
and stillness
steps into the air behind her.

The weight she cannot feel but as a pulse
of unexpected modesty
is only our attention resting
beside her in the holly garden.

Tasselled nettles, ivy with its frog-shaped leaves,
are seeking what they most resemble.

Solvitur ambulando.

Drops of water on the leaves of holly
remind her of fragility:
but all at once the hopelessness
her erstwhile husband, Dr Pordage, calls
'a little seasonal depression'
seems light enough for all such surfaces.

In Jesmond, her thesis on the pastoral mode
awaits completion
in black bin-liners by a makeshift desk.

XIII

Come, let us goe, while we are in our prime,
and take the harmless follie of the time.

Our one flesh, Marjorie,
that was a chandler's wife at Hexham,
had pissed my mother's bed in drink
the night they put me to her.

Last and my father preached extempore
and my flesh rose.

What God has cleansed, call thou not uncleane.

XIV

With little interruption by its islands,
the Indian Ocean
vastly folds and smooths its rigs.

Beach fires of the heathen raise
a level smoke veil
that separates the sea-flats and the bastion,
and laden barges from the masts at anchor.

Within a cannon-shot of Fort St George,
a resting ox looks up at whip crack,
another, and a distant cry,
to witness English law enacted.

My father ploughed with oxen still
the cloud-swabbed slope below The Orchard,
before the sheep came everywhere
and Richard Last began to preach and print
the blood that crieth in the ears.

His rigs are there for evening sun to notice
as if a grassy main had clenched
the farm, and that become a wrecked stone ship,
its cargo sunk into the moor.

The sea forgives the keel its furrow.

XV

The treasure came to port at London,
and then aboard a collier vessel
pertaining to Sir William Blackett, Baronet,
and then by cart from Newcastle.

That, I myself was witness to.

There is a little sparke lies under
thine honour, pomp and riches,
which shall consume, as it is written.

XVI

Howl, howl, ye nobles, howl honourable,
for the miseries that come upon you.

Is your face towards the light?

Even a tendril of the rose-bush
the night wind stirs against your wall
will leave a groove an axe might cut.

Together, remember, we have cauled
the youth I was
in darkness and a pedlar's pack,
while time in Lee Hall kitchen ticks
three hundred years
against the measure of my heart.

Are you in trembling of a rich man's clock?

Consider the spine of one great tree,
its branches lopped, its saw cut vertebrae
tumbled into English grass.

For our parts, wee'l have all things common,
wee'l break our bread from house to house.

XVII

The housemaid's whisper frightens me.

Come, our wanderer is a shepherdess
whose thoughts are grazing
in sunlit parkland, where a fine grey house
stands back politely,
paid-for out of coal and lead.

Passion plucks no berries
from the myrtle and ivy
nor calls upon Arethuse and Mincius,
nor tells of rough satyrs, and fauns
with cloven heel...

Trim nails against the texture of her page
prevent a breeze from turning it.

Is this thy love, thy dove, thy fair one?

Consoling emblems slip my mind,
and she has closed her eyes to see them:
the salmon in its pelt of light,
the treasure cart,
and then the very last I saw
before tarred cloth enveloped me,
a white bull, motionless
against the gathered and substantial dark
of Houxty Wood,
and the moon and stars in ecstasy.

I must not move.

XVIII

Claude's pictures fade, and leave your window
locked darkly on Northumberland.

Chesterhope's a muddy doormat:
you are a poem-spider trod thereon.

What have we then? A revelation?
Or normal untruth soaking bones
of whinstone in a bleating mist?

There's more to pastoral than meets the eye.

XIX

My honeymoon left me a widower:
a mourner at an empty grave, moreover,
and still the priest to pay.

As high of heart as she would ride of old,
Helen, who that wild day in death's despite
escaped the durance of the churchyard mould.

Thus I have also known despair.

XX

How will you meet her, by the way?

She reads the papers. You could try,
sincere male wishes (ho ho)
for friendship and outings (ha ha).

No no.

Be wise now therefore. O ye Rulers
be instructed. Give over, give over
thy midnight mischief.

A chance encounter might be engineered.

A pilgrimage to see the Templars' mark
where Derwentwater's brother, of the Prieuré,
may pensively have placed his fingers.

You could share that.

A sound like rain across the dry church roof,
or one short cry from empty shrubbery,
might get you talking in that haunted place.

XXI

This is your summer, and the oak tree
grips its leaves about my face.

The last Leveller that was shot to death:
a face of leaves
that stares back smiling at your own.

It took five tons of oak to smelt one ton
of iron, a skelp of land to feed one sheep.

For you, we ranting Angels might have turned
oak roots in the wards of earth
to unlock England for her cheated yeomanry.

The very shadow frighted you
and shook your kingdome.

Rout out the titled man in every hollow,
unfurling park land, dunning for his rents!

The substantiality of levelling is comming.

XXII

Sinne and transgression is finisht,
a meere riddle, that they
with all their humane learning cannot reade.

North Tyne, untarnished by the moon, I see
still flows stealthily by Houxty. A shield
of pasture there may yet contain
the like of that heraldic bull
whose glimmering stillness strengthened me, the night
we wove our stratagem within the wood.

Alan, that was my lost bride Helen's brother,
my father, busy as a gnat,
poor drunken Marjorie: their divers ends
I cannot know. Together with myself,
whose death you must be privy to,
this was our one flesh dwindled to its remnant.

Some beer, some scraps of bread and meat, a sword,
two knives, and one great pistol
my father brandished like the cuddy's jawbone
Samson hefted, owning neither shot nor powder:
these, with my silver whistle and a Bible,
comprised our final commonwealth.

Thou and thy Family are fed,
as the young ravens strangely.

XXIII

Then, since we mortal lovers are,
ask not how long our love will last;
but while it does, let us take care
each minute be with pleasure passed.

Her boots and anorak
are in the kitchen with a residue
of spaghetti carbonara, cheese and apples,
and Côtes du Roussillon Villages.

She's heard of Rennes le Château and the Prieuré,
and shares your view
across Greenrigg to Derwentwater's stone
and light withdrawing.

I see that she herself removes,
after her dungarees and Oxfam jumper,

surprisingly upmarket underwear
and helps you slip into the grateful place
last occupied by Dr Pordage.

Did Daphnis and his nymph, or Danaë
beneath her shower of gold enjoy
such raptures in Arcadia?

XXIV

Twigs drawn in half-dark from my father's fist
decide our parts: Alan shall play
the stout cajoling pedlar, I, with fierce
and silent eloquence, his burden.

We have, of rope and canvas taken
by stealth from Marjorie's chandler's yard,
sufficiency, though it be foul.

Lee Hall is Troy, its garrison
a housemaid and a gardener
who wags a blunderbuss named Copenhagen.

Deliver, deliver,
my money that thou hast to rogues,
whores and cut-purses, who are flesh of thy flesh,
or els by my selfe, saith the Lord,
I will torment thee day and night.

Colonel Ridley's heathen treasure
will buy us passage to America
and land for freeborn Angels to rejoice in.

An unkind wind
strews silver on the river's velvet
counter like a money lender.

XXV

Give over thy base and stinking formall grace
before and after meat, give over
thy nasty, stinking family duties,
thy Gospell Ordinances;
for under them lies snarling, snapping,
biting, covetousnesse, evill surmising,
envy, malice, and horrid hypocrisie.

Give over, or if nothing els will do it,
I'l make thy child, in whom thy soul delighted,
lie with a whore before thine eyes.

By that base thing, that plaguy holinesse
and righteousnesse of thine shall be confounded,
and thou plagued back, damned and rammed
into thy mother's womb that is Eternity.

Then thou shall see no evill furthermore
but rather one huge beauty,
but first lose righteousness and holinesse
and every crum of thy Religion.

XXVI

Your duck-down duvet jerks and slides.

Now I can address you both. Outside,
thin snow sheets a whinstone bed.

Is my borrowed voice too faint? Too loud?

I fear I am no better hand
at haunting than at levelling:
beneath my slab, a bone-cache

tangled in the yew tree's roots,
I wait for recognition and for naming
while witnessing my own conception.

Ther's my riddle.

My hinny in her poor bunched shroud,
thrown from the lathered back of Heatherbell,
had the swan-begotten queen for namesake,
and yet still waits for burial
unless a mine or hag received her.

I know that beasts more easily return,
their souls more apt,
as Heatherbell the roan came back
to haunt The Orchard for the apple
your new love gave her.

Feare thou not,
creep forth a little in this mystery.

XXVII

Time rattles in the ewe's throat
and time would faile if I would tell you all.

I saw diversity, variety, distinction
and as clearly saw
all folded into Unity,
and that has been my song since then.

The dead do not know who they are
until they are remembered.

XXVIII

She steps towards me in the early morning.

A lantern flares, and Copenhagen utters
the word that lifts me
above the stink of my own blood.

My cloth womb splits.

In Houxty Wood,
mist turns to smallest rain to make
visible a shift of air
that tilts the faces of the leaves.

She kneels, unwary
as she quickens, finding pipe-ash lichen,
oyster lichen, tiny rubies
delightful on my narrow stone.

It was thus resembled,
as if a great brush dipt in whiting
should sweep a picture off a wall.

The voice you hear has made itself your child.

The Border

To stop and gaze here is to worship
and then, by worshipping, to close the gap
that falls between us and the pulse of things.

This is the veritable border.

When I was young they called the place a book
that presses us between its pages.

Not everyone is happy here.

Some are fearful of our agile language
that crouches just beyond their understanding:
the concert of our streams and woods,
our singing flowers.

Our staple product now is marvels:
the man, for instance, up the valley,
who grows new clothes upon himself in summer
with something itchy in the lining
that makes him shrug them off each winter.

Fairytale

The children dream a foray, and their bodies
follow on their hands and knees
out from the forest, under barbed wire fences.

The wind among the trees is scolding.

A company of white geese by the stream,
down where the lane goes through a farmyard
overhung and dark with oaks,
are moonlit so that they resemble
excisions from an older, radiant world.

These are dream geese, docile, and too beautiful
to raise their wings in clamour, or to scatter.

Breath keeps pace as bare soles, gladdening
to soft damp earth and smell of prey,
accelerate a measured run,
and this is good, and this is human nature.

Wolf-girls, wolf-boys, spread your arms
find balance, vocalise your hunger.

Each night the geese are there again, but stronger.

Inyuyucoy

At night, there is a kind of creature here
that has an eye of light, a radiance
you would not think could grace the world.

Wait, and it will enter from the garden,
its plumage swishing, on all fours,
and full of love and information.

This beast does not endure abuse or capture,
because it baffles all designs
by sudden darkness, or by sudden dazzle.

When love and news have been acknowledged,
you'll see it flop asleep upon the carpet,
its splendour veiled, like furniture
you never meant to have in your possession.

Woodsmoke

after Piero di Cosimo

Whoever stands as you do at this window,
looking out from where you are exactly,
will see the things that you see start to happen.

Sky-shapes that hang between the trees
catch light like dawn, but dawn too early
to wake the pigeons or the calling crane.

The forest kindles, filling up with voices
that sing in tune with your attention.

Then something like the sunrise comes, and men
disguised as animals run out towards you
and fall, but after falling rise
as animals like you, disguised as men.

The Little Flame

Here is the place, and where they kept
his childhood in a locked room off the kitchen.

You still require a chair to reach
the key upon its hook above the dresser.

This window is the one at which he saw
the little flame that crept down from the woods
above the house, the night before
they stopped believing what he had to tell them.

Nothing is reliable or modern,
but sunset has arrived to tint the fleeces
of flocks that do not fear the wolf or lion,
and life here will be good with decent plumbing,
an Aga, and sufficient time
to warm the world you're ready to imagine.

The Punt *Nixie*

The river can be unrelenting
when no one says: let's get back home
and not tie up here and begin to whisper
so close against the ear of sunset
with ground mist rising in the nearer fields.

You classify experience by colour,
and what you tell me in your greyest voice
concerns grey streams, grey swimmers in them,
and how your secret life is grey,
shot through with pain like red light on the water.

All this is difficult to disentangle
in twilight, under willow branches.

Uncle George and the Snow Bunting

Finches among hawthorn berries,
and then the quickness of a yellowhammer,
refresh him, and the wren that flies
unerringly within the hedge
next to the lane below the rectory.

Without a sound, meanwhile, he enters
the wood, beside the keeper's gibbet.

Along the margin of an unpaid bill
that bears a butcher's thumbprint, like a seal,
he lists the leaf-like scraps of moles and squirrels,
weasels, stoats, a whiff of rotting,
black feathers and the beaks of crows,
a magpie with its tail in tatters,
the speckled breasts of sparrowhawks and kestrels,
their voided eyes, two tawny owls
revolving as a slight wind moves.

Tirrip, chiss-ick, chiss-ick, tee-ewe.

Inside his hat there is a winter bird
he went in search of once, that flutters
through snowflakes like a butterfly
in places hard to climb to and austere,
but pretty in those fading sketches
he brought back from his student holiday.

Lead, kindly Light, amid the encircling gloom,
  Lead thou me on;
The night is dark, and I am far from home;
  Lead thou me on.

It's hard to have much patience with a ghost
that shrivels to such earnestness:
his wretched socks, his narrow boots, the rain
his sombre clothes soak up, the pain
of fast-receding faith, all these remain
Victorian, as solemnly perverse
as long repining for a love unspoken.

And yet what strength it had, that piety
with which chums down from varsity
sang Newman to the frosty air, and, later,
how strong the hope that brings him seeking
those linked arms as he falls through time, and laughter.

The Fossil

She knows that it is risky, nowadays,
woken by chance and in the dark,
not to keep herself in focus.

Last night she had been slithering
back into the quarry basin,
the thick green water and the jewelled silt.

She thinks of people and professions
there to help her, in their fashion.

She thinks of sweet, unconscious preservation
in sediment, her life a gem
of which she only knows the special virtue.

Is she a bat-like thing? A hippogriff?

The self she had not thought she could remember
has left a path to be completed.

She sees again, in landscape squeezed of light,
her early footprints, each claw perfect,
blurring, then in turn unblurring,
in thin dust drifting at the quarry's rim.

The Damp Harmonium

The sea is cold, the moon is veiled,
and clouds are frantic with the coming storm.

A salt-bleached stile leads down to where
the graveyard is, and milky foam
embroiders rocks, as rising swell
attacks the shore and falls back, breaking.

Tonight a ship must surely founder.

The only craftsman on the island
has cut down every tree there was,
and now he is reduced to driftwood
to make his souvenirs and toys
and all the coffins in his workshop.

It's true that here we see the world
as if it were a long way off
until the ocean brings it closer.

The village hall is furnished as a chapel:
the minister has long departed
and yet his congregation comes
unsummoned at the hour of worship.

The storm breaks and the lamps grow dim.

See how the drowned have filled the doorway,
incandescent in their youth and beauty,
and how the damp harmonium is gleeful.

Please stand and join us as we raise our voices
to sing the island's only hymn.

The Pigeon Loft

No doubt you will have heard of his remark
that firelight on a darkened window
resembled all that seemed to stand
between him and the fecund, various world
from out of which his powers came.

He was adept at obfuscation.

He also may have said that music flies
into the ears on small black wings:
but attribution there is shaky.

Somehow, during his sojourn in Prague,
he found material for those delusions
for which his short career is now remembered.

We are unlikely to discover,
behind the smoke-clouds and dark instruments,
where exactly research led him,
or what he let loose in the pigeon loft.

He earned a bonfire for himself, that's clear
if you examine the aghast expression
he wears in that last woodcut, or the knock-
kneed verses of his *True Confession*.

The Sisters

Broad steps with parapets ascend
from waste ground where the slicks reflect
streetlights near the underpass.

Leaping arches and emblazoned glass
confront the backs of factories.

A dwarf is bowing in embroidered flounces.

He leads us through impossible apartments:
one houses minerals, another pictures,
and farther on there's china, bronzes.

Here is the Cedar Boudoir, where the sisters
approached delirium, with even
their most minute and common parts
hand-crafted into ornament.

Outside, the buses have stopped running.

A dog I do not like trots with me,
his collar richly stitched with emblems
I am unwilling to bend down to see.

Squiffy

This trek has been like never learning,
with every step the same mistake,
and something vital left behind
among the trees, down where the fever swarms
vibrate beneath the heavy leaves.

What he's been looking for is there, abruptly,
and then the mountain elbows out the view.

Yes, there it is again, the shimmering house,
with its verandah in a wedge of dark,
tethered to its track out from the bush.

There is no sign of cooking-smoke, or cattle,
no dog is barking in the stable-yard.

The air is still, the midday light impartial.

It's time for him to start the long descent
towards the camp-bed in the shade, the gramophone.

It's strange how one idea sticks in his head.

It's nothing, really, only a daftness:
like the chap who once, back home, got squiffy
and fought a goblin on the vicar's lawn.

Breathe Carefully

In your attic there could be a shrouded globe,
some tinsel, flashbulbs, and a picture book.

If not, some bobbins and a rocking horse,
or, better still, an old piano stool,
a dusty window, and a dying moth:
it doesn't matter, work with what you find,
so long as you have all you need for stitching.

When you see the man-shape and its shadow,
look right through them, make the voice of thunder.

The job, of course, must not remain too solid.

Peel off one dimension, make it flat
enough to slide the whole thing sideways
into the future of your certain person,
precisely when he turns away abruptly,
dismissing you, and is not mindful
of your importance, his fragility.

If this seems difficult, go back
and practise basic wrapping and unfolding.

Nothing is achieved without expenditure:
before you start, try emptying your purse
into an unfamiliar ditch or culvert
while snow falls, and the beggars are in shelter.

Breathe carefully, a little at a time,
unhook the phone, and bolt your door.

The Intervention

Now that we have made the aperture
between the pillow and the head, we can
quite easily insert a panorama.

Tonight I think we'll use the estuary
together with a dreamy landscape,
reflecting back the setting sun.

It is traditional, but most effective.

The patient will remember vast
receding distances, and yet
they are of course minute from our perspective.

Nightmares that congregate to kiss
their own reflections as they stoop to drink
present the only problem with this option.

We must allow time for their games
of hide-and-seek and writhing hurly-burly,
before they vanish from the shallows
to merge with stillness and the rosy light.

At this point do not dilly-dally.

If we are slow to make the intervention,
then we may lose the patient at the instant
that sunset starts to leave the water
in darkness to become the river
that is too wide and deep for us to cross.

Ogress

You think I only cook, and clean, and launder?

I used to yoke the oxen, and the elephant,
to pull his wheelchair to the height
through veils of rain, so he could watch
the playful mountains throwing rocks
until the valleys shook their sides
and all the beasts ran from the woods.

He has been known to curdle frost
on winter mornings with a look, and yet
that spectacle could sometimes make him smile.

Your little world would no doubt condescend
to laugh at this, and at our oddity –
his size, my warty skin and single eye –
but no one comes here now, and laughter,
so unbecoming in the well-brought-up,
is never heard in these grey vastnesses.

He should have recognised his own good luck.

I did not need him to inform me
how well I suit my situation
by virtue of monstrosity,
when I considered it a privilege
to serve him while I could, unstintingly.

His punishment is now to drag his body
up marble stairs alone, night after night,
each riser higher than the last, each step
with what he owes me carved into the tread.

Listening Duty

Last night she told me all about the house
that dances: its façades
turquoise and lime, sometimes magenta,
changing colour as it bobs and twirls
away from England and its damp, grey light.

You can imagine her, I'm sure,
small and exotic in the well
of that high room above the bomb-sites
and moonlit porticoes:
Belgravia, with blackout paint
still covering the windows on the stairs.

Her background-story doesn't gel,
and yet I can detect a pattern
that always pulls us in the same direction.

Tonight, before I go off listening-duty,
the check-points and the customs-sheds
of Europe will be up and dancing,
and policemen, in their heavy boots.

The Banner Men

From burned-out granaries and fuel dumps
come whisperings of pain and rage,
while dogs are gnawing battle scraps
and starving as their fleas increase.

Behind this coastal plain, the sombre
hinterland wears combat dress: low walls collapse
beside the ditches they were quarried from,
and turrets shift on steeps of rubble.

Ours is a virile and a martial age.

The man who knows the routes the convoys use
has built his palace out of twisted metal,
betrayed by clues outside the entrance tunnel:
some bubblegum, a playing card, and sputum.

His job is mending roads, for which
he hopes some government may yet reward him,
meanwhile he has hot news to barter.

He is a craftsman, and prepared to forage
for sculpture or for lettered stone,
like that with extracts from our Constitution,
or, when he can, for loot from old museums
that represents female fecundity
or gods and goddesses from cinemas.

Look how his hammer splits the face
of that fine marble Mickey Mouse,
and, as he tamps them in position,
how well the grinning fragments fit the camber.

Spare him, my brothers, while he keeps his watch.

The love of beauty dignifies his labour,
and, like we banner men, he will not grovel
or farm the land, and that is noble.

Ride on, and burn what junk he has,
yet, of our magnanimity,
allow him life for art, which is no more
or less than we enjoy, whose art is slaughter,
though we gain banners and the spoils of war.

The Imp

Watch how you go, the path down there
is blocked in parts by builders' rubble,
and slippy under rotting leaves.

The house is cramped but neat, and both
the parents of the imp are solid folk,
the father clever with his hands, the mother
not knowing how to let herself be idle.

Encourage them in conversation.

They will speak proudly of its horns and tail
and rough skin, caustic to the touch.

I'll be astonished if you fail
to find the fixity of their devotion
comforting, in some ways, to the mind.

If you intend to make a close inspection,
present my compliments, and take
your gardening gloves and overalls,
and something for the lad himself, perhaps
a horseshoe for a teething-ring.

The Cypher

The air is thick up through the wood
but not oppressive in the central clearing.

You may admire what stands there all the better
for stepping forward into freshness,
and contemplate my work with no discomfort.

No Gothick flights remain, since your remarks
in your kind missive, which I have to hand,
not even the encircling verandah
I had myself contrived, for which
I nursed an artist's fondness, I confess,
together with the four tripartite arches,
the balcony, the quatrefoil and fluted friezes.

Instead, we have a domed and pillared building,
strict in design, with simple capitals
above which is *RESURGAM* and the cypher,
exactly in accordance with your wishes.

The iron door is open, as you see.

My men thought that to close it, in this weather,
except you were yourself, Sir, placed within,
might prompt the tempest, and, when all was finished,
draw down upon their heads a thunderbolt.

The Sally Garden

Become a puppy once again
and leave your half-chewed catalogue
of wasted chances on the rug
of snug regrets and snuff the sweet
night air among the sally trees.

Gaps in the stonework of the wall, and ivy
entangled in the trellises,
seem etched by moonlight to provide
good lodgements for your teeth and paws.

I see you also now have hands and toes.

Once up, reach for the sally boughs and tug
yourself towards me while I set your feet
upon the stone head of Mnemosyne.

She's mossy, but securely placed
for you to slither down, into the fog
of what was once a paradise.

Let's see no sadness in your eyes.

I have arranged some things of yours
together in a single thought:
an awful childhood and a spade
left in the ground to rust, and scars
of earth amid the wilderness,
as if someone with half a mind
to find a good spot for a grave had dug
without conviction, or a dog
had half remembered where a bone was laid.

The Angel

The snow is feather-like and slow descending
between the spires, and now the room
itself begins to fill with feathers
that glow and give off sounds and odours.

Put down your notebook: pass the lamp.

This is an outcome we must spare
no time or labour to suppress.

Up through the neck comes speech, the damp
core only of each vocable,
and then that diffident, sweet-natured smile
returns as if it can remember,
each time it tries to lift a wing
from off the rag rug by the study fire,
the outspread heavens, like a curtain.

Our colleagues will endorse our course of action.

This creature is too frail to bear –
pull back my shirt cuffs if you will, Professor –
our human narrowness of range and know
each hour it lives that it must die,
and meanwhile drag its feet through slush, and never
ascend in splendour into falling snow.

Miss Daphne

Show me those lower teeth, she said,
mouths wide, your lips well down, and sing.

We sang more like a pulse, so pure
our teacher's face put off its urging,
becoming younger in the garden,
more like an answer, a decision made.

She took her clothes off then, and danced.

That's how it was, a drowsy sound,
our lips well down, our open mouths,
while she danced all the woodland creatures
and one slim tree whose shape she has
to this day, by the summer-house.

JIGGER NODS

Warner, whose immortal pen
praised every honest Englishman
that strives to set old Albion free
from giants of adversity,
founded our school and built our rule
in good Queen Bess's reign.

The Founder's Anthem

We think no greater blisse than such
to be as be we would,
when blessèd none but such as be
the same as be they should.

WILLIAM WARNER, *Albion's England*

I

Is it still visible, the bright
imaginary green,
within this future we are moving to?

Jigger sees it, all a dazzle,
beyond the monkeypuzzle tree.

II

Wind, time, and sun reel shadows back
to flicker over market stalls
towards the coke-works and the shunting yard,
a greasy café wedged beneath an arch,
and hinterland where sooty hills are dozing.

There, in that town, are the fleet of foot,
the armoured and the many-headed.

Stables brim and reek, a thousand
inky essays wait for marking,
and amazons rebuff him, one by one,
except Hippolytë, who leaves
her girdle on the field of battle.

Ex pede Herculem!

The world is worse than it was then,
thinks Jigger, with a crooked troupe
of immigrants and nancy-boys
exploiting Albion, and grinding down
the spirit of her Englishmen.

III

For many years he livèd thus,
stipended so to live,
and shepherd-like to teach a flock
himself did wholly give...

Put your feet up, Hercules.

An armchair, whisky, and a smoke,
improve the taste of goading boys
towards a rumour of applause
that's fainter as the years go by
and banish thoughts of Iphicles,
the boy your mother loved the best,
who was her husband's only son.

No need to struggle with the tall sash now.

Outside the eighteen darkening panes
lies all the sorrow of the Masters' Garden,
where beehives and exotic trees
are spectral in the mist that hides
the empty playing-fields, and then
the valley's steeper banks, its flow.

IV

It's safer to be drunk than think.

What was that certainty, the day
he crumpled as his wife confessed
the focus of her restlessness,
then beat a slithery retreat
in hobnails and a waterproof,
that he had somehow glimpsed himself,

androgynous and beckoning,
a long way off across a planted field?

Thought salvaged him, and it was merely
a scarecrow in a cotton dress.

V

Boys barge from fart-filled rooms, and men
on tiptoe from the common-room
leave Jigger to his lonely ease
as something frets the outside dark
and taps the glass as if to enter.

O zonam perdidit!

Somewhere today he lost the key
that swung in pain-inflicting arcs
inside the long sleeve of his chalky gown.

His Latin tags are fatuous.

Ozone is what he needs, not drink,
perchance a holiday, meanwhile
his spectacles are gone, his books, his pen
that cut with scarlet *ynke*:
schoolmastering hits heads of only
the shadows of its silly boys.

VI

Brute suppressed the Albinests,
huge giants, fierce and strong,
and of this isle, un-Scotted yet,
he empire had ere long…

When Jigger nods and dreams the end
of titan Albion and all
his upstart swarthy Albinests,
he sees true Albion, the land, released,
eponymous, that Trojan Brute
and all fair-skinned, fair-minded Brutons
may tramp in peace their native hills.

Such views were rife when he attended
the University of Troy Novant.

VII

Recall that morning, spiked with pot-pourri,
when sunlight and suburban air,
asked only that he knuckle down
to make sense of that how-do-you-do
of lipstick messages, the rage
of underwear Hippolytë
took off with her and twice the man
that he was then, black-skinned and ardent,
borne up on U.S. airforce wings.

For as the Smith with hammers beats
his forgèd metal, so
he dubs his club about their pates
and fleas them in a row...

Those other mornings were more happy,
when, hopping to avoid the plop,
he swished a stick, bold *claviger*,
to shoo the big cat on the farmyard wall,
while Deianira, Iole, and Hebe,
led the herd, with flailing tails,
down towards the dangerous pasture
that held the river and the anglers' hut,

to leave him swinging on the gate, an imp
in wellingtons, not merely Henry
but one the vicar, on his jovial way,
would call his infant Hercules.

VIII

Her upper parts had humaine forme,
her nether Serpentine,
the whole was monstrous, yet her wit
more monstrous, was most fine…

A spring within the armchair twangs.

It seems the scarecrow has begun
to add to beckoning a voice
that undermines his snug, well-worn regret
that he is old and drunk already
and never was an Oxford man.

IX

Now the door is not quite shut.

A need is scratching to come in, an itch
for more than that corrosive fable
of blowing roadside oaks and elms
and gates in hedgerows that reveal
those gleaming meadows, snowy orchards,
and parks in which ancestral piles
stand, among great-hearted timber,
for all that Dornford Yates and Jigger
think Englishness amounts to in the end.

Here comes a question and a wounding
that wakes him to confront the dark.

Eheu fugaces… labuntur anni!

Outside, each fallen leaf records
the grieving of the arboretum.

X

Alas that from the lab stinks rise.

Boy-haunted passages are glooming fast:
no time to ogle photographs
of First XIs, First XVs,
or keep an eye on changing rooms.

Aut insanit homo aut versus facit!

Yes, Sir, we know that you eschewed
perverse insanitary deeds.

XI

Just like the spook in Betton Wood,
or Alfred's child, the scarecrow speaks
but has no language but a cry
that makes her grinning topknot tremble
above the snake-shreds of her frock.

He sees the flutter of her hesitation
positioned where a cloud adjusts
and readjusts, as in a loop,
the envelope of light in which
she seems unable to complete
the half-turn she has almost made.

Obscurum per obscurius!

Perhaps she calculates the cost
of entry to a human heart,
and, scenting lack of will, resolves
to try her skill at bilocation.

Her cut-throat grin becomes a gap
between the inner and the outer dark
through which thin mischief starts to seep.

XII

The black man, grinning as he mounts a wing
to reach the cockpit of his plane,
has bleached to buff before he falls
off the locker, by the bed
in which Hippolytë is doped asleep,
and shatters glass and no one sees
the cleaner bin him, fearing censure.

GOODBYE TO DR IPHICLES

A photo from the local paper
is also quickly binned, compressed
to pellet-form and lobbed by Jigger.

It shows the town's most popular GP
beside his wife and smiling colleagues,
multiracial, un-class-conscious,
for *au-revoirs* before he flies
to serve in long-postponed retirement
with Médecins Sans Frontières.

XIII

The hives are sleeping, and no honey bees
could replicate what he can hear
outside his window, in the monkeypuzzle.

It is a sibilance that scarecrows find
torments the kind of men who look
at women as into a mirror
to see the face of what they loathe.

It's not just women Jigger trusts
to make him squirm, but all their flock
of nancy-boys and fancy-men,
and jungle-monkeys on the make,
and Celtic whingers with their paws
about the throat of Albion.

To lacke life lost in chalke and ynke:
an hell, an hell, an hell…

A time has come when what he hates
is coiled so tight about his chest
that fear and rage unreconciled
grow hot enough to scorch his vest.

The lilac waits beside the oak.

More subtle than the ghosts of ghosts
are all the causes in their ancient files
of what he is, and must now lose.

XIV

Does he still hope for company?

Then fill an afternoon with summer heat,
the breathy rub of thirty boys,
the shipboard creak of desks, the creep
of Platignum and Osmiroid.

Is there a danger to the perfect grass?

Jerk up the window, out with him and under,
arms and legs a movie flicker,
to kite his black and tattered sleeves
towards the shimmering cricket square
where, in the haze, dark limbs and creamy
entwine in ecstasy unnoticed
by men who mow, and mark the creases.

How fair she was, and who she was,
she bore for him the bell
that knew although he clownish is
the place where beauty dwells…

Such moments hold the hours and years.

Wake up the organ with the Founder's Anthem,
let sunlight play on beeswaxed floors
and trophies, mustered in a silver dazzle
as if for battle, and a raft of flowers.

Have sashes squeak, and schoolboy faces
cling like sediment to sills and sides
of lofty windows, eighteen-paned,
to see a burnished car deposit,
to comic bugles of the Corps, and birdsong

never heard so clearly since,
a royal duchess, polka-dotted,
with long silk gloves whose fingers reach
down forty years to squeeze his fingers.

Non nisi malis terrori!

Beneath her condescending smile,
thin sticks are what her dress hangs on.

XV

The sooty hills have shuffled off
their weight of visibility:
allotments where the town expires
are compartmentalising dusk.

As quick as breath, let's be aboard
the train home through a fading day.

Each night, cold lights of combines turn
to shave straight edges of the crop
then turn again: hauled in their wake,
jolting balers pack the hay.

XVI

Whose so-called father's room, whose bed,
is where this broken breathing comes?

Bis pueri senes!

This lad should not be here at all
alone at this late early time,
the stillest of a summer night,

when childhood ends with harvest baled
and scattered in the stubble fields.

He should not stand too near this window
or dare to breathe such altered air.

Fear and freedom are his chums,
clasp-knife-wielding, boy-scout-belted,
with bread and jam in greaseproof paper,
to track adventure to its lair
in full sun of the holidays,
out by the pungent path next to the lilac
and the wide trunk of the climbing oak,
in which, among the highest branches,
his tattered kite is bravely flapping:
heraldic, irretrievable. Perhaps.

The bedside tick, the bedside tock,
are louder when the breathing stops.

XVII

I'll leave here when that monkeypuzzle
puts out one bloody English rose.

The worse for booze, a breathless grip
comes back as if his chest belonged
to him no longer, but a man
who dies each night, or else a son
he might have been, an Iphicles
whose decent, hopeful heart expands too far.

The best of bees do beare, beside
sweet honey, smarting stings,
and time doth not need any baite
that unto sorrow brings…

And not until the lawyer finds
a legacy for Iphicles
and none for him, and only then
is Jigger sent to make his claim
upon the doorstep of the vicarage,
before the tall door in the rain,
on one who kept his mother mum
and will bequeath him nothing but her blame.

XVIII

Silence strikes its longest note.

Time dawdles where the scarecrow flickers,
as if projected through an inner lens,
and guys him, done up like a sailor's floozy,
while Christmas holidays repeat, and summers
go by with minor maintenance:
the school asleep through tinker shuffles
late every morning of the mops and pails.

More bloody darkies every term.

What wakes the hives among the leaves
that scab the lawn like dead skin dropping?

Again the pain recedes, and whisky
dilates his throat the more to croak
his mockery of banter,
not laughable, an obstacle to laughter.

The loop snaps and the scarecrow moves.

XIX

The whole was monstrous, yet her wit,
more monstrous, was most fine,
and fed on fear and spite she thus
confounded all she found,
propounding questions, and a word
unanswered was a wounde...

Heart thuds that activate the air
like tiny eddies of departure
disturb the room and silence prompts
echoes, barely short of stillness,
which are inquisitorial.

How noiselessly the tall sash rises.

She's found your bolt-hole, Henry Jigger,
master of the sleepy arts
of armchair and tobacco jar,
by way of ramblers' paths and roads
turned serpentine, and boy-scuffed rooms,
and labs and halls and corridors,
and trees and hives where mist conceals
what slithers in the Masters' Garden.

XX

If only once, he should have skipped
behind the herd into the morning sun
that tipped their horns with gold, and turned,
as Warner sings, a crab, perhaps,
or tuned a round to test the air
as far as to the farthest pasture,
boldly heedless of comeuppance.

Dum vivimus, vivamus!

Likewise, the necessary grit
to be a comrade to a restless wife,
and fund a family and find it later,
if not quite grateful, well disposed,
might now have helped him face the dark
and dust that settles all he chose.

They sweetly surfeiting in joy
and silent for a space,
whenas the ecstacy had end
did tenderly embrace.

An hell then, speechless Vivimus?

Its topknot level with the open window,
in murk that thickens as he peers
to see what something outside is,
the araucaria extends its fingers
to shelter nothing, and to shed no leaves.

XXI

Alas, the fleeting years, alas
the nursing home that drearily
accommodates Hippolytë
and swindles Dr Iphicles.

She and her twice-the-man, now unremembered,
share their lost time with the zephyr
that makes the scarecrow beckon, and forever
disturbs the tassel on the mortarboard
of Jigger by the the royal car,
the day he hears the organ grumble
in concert with the bugles and the birds.

Hebe, Iole, and Deianira,
for the last time in that selfsame moment
re-enter the forbidden pasture.

That no-time, neither tick nor tock,
is at the window when poor Jigger
falls as if he falls for ever
from childhood into altered air.

Necessitas non habet legem!

For leglessness, a final dram
is once again what we require.

XXII

He is too pusillanimous
upon this second windowsill
to trust the voice that calls him out
to play the man and earn his wings
above the fives court and the Bursar's house,
the shut pavilion and the stud-pocked fields.

But Hercules is brave and young
among the footholds of the oak
whose branches close and then fall back
before his blows, bold *claviger*,
until his black kite lifts away
its academical and chalky tatters,
to clamber up the playful sky.

XXIII

It's Jigger's turn to spook the eye:
his bee-swarm of the heart becomes
a palanquin that bears him up
like Brutus into Albion
above the tree-tops of the Masters' Garden
triumphally, then lets him drop.

The hives vibrate.

A tattered tongue uncoils and spits
while polka-dots of dapples fall
in strange light where a shive of summer
warms the duchess in the arboretum,
her snake-shreds sloughed, and wearing daisies
entangled in her pubic hair,
for waggle-dancing, and the splits.

So who can equal Hercules
by whom the monster fell
who, burning up her ugly shape,
did passe her soule to hell?

Tonight Her Royal Highness finds
herself the lithe embodiment
of lewd and ludicrous delight, wherefrom
the voice proceeds that soothes the bees.

XXIV

Contraries be the elements,
at strife contraries fall,
yeat Sea, the Earth, the Aier, them both,
the skie be-cleaps them all...

In the café, therefore greasy, stirring
as trains pass, hangs the banner of St George
above the palid bone-shaved heads of Brutons.

On hinterland where hills are dark and soggy
and neighbourhoods where black and white
share terraces by railway-lines,
a mosque, a synagogue, and many churches,
on market stalls of jeans and saris,
and softly on the flat-roofed day-room
in which, upon a high-seat chair,
Hippolytë is sitting, dreaming,
autumn dampness turns to drizzle.

Meanwhile, a strange unlovely rose,
blood-scumbled, will be stretchered down
and pouched among the fallen leaves.

Recreant wretch, he Albion loved
and wished her to be free,
that causèd him to suffer on
a cruel outlandish tree…

Across the lawn, three policewomen,
Iole, Deianira, Hebe,
as if in mourning, gather clothes,
a hearing-aid and shoes, a watch-chain,
in line with a trajectory
a jump for England might have barely managed
from window-sill to monkeypuzzle.

Your native rain, O Hercules, dissolves
the Hydra's venom in the blood
and cools at last your fiery vest.

XXV

Nor meete it were, in Justice or
in nature, things of nought
shall equal that unbounded Power
that All of Nothing wrought.

That be not Two or divers Gods
is also prompt by this,
and vanitie is Period
of everie thing that is.

Of One all Multiplicities,
Formes, Harmonies, (what not?)
be, howsoere they seeme confused,
producèd and begot.

Of whichsoere all creatures be
compounded formally,
so then of contrarieties
is Uniformitie.

To one Sea flow all Fluds, one Sunne
inlighteneth every Light,
of all celestiall Movings is
one Mover, artists write.

Trunke, barke, boughs, leaves, and blossomes, none
like others hath a Tree,
yet but one Roote, whence all, which but
one Author's act can bee.

XXVI

Somewhere a bell, elsewhere a morning
choir is on its feet and singing:

Behold a teacher, with the Sun
he doth his flocke engage
and all the day with ynke and chalk
he merry warre can wage,
and with the Sun doth fold again,
then jogging home betime,
he turns a crab, or tunes a round,
or sings some merry rhyme…

Warner's verse, the driest work
committed yet to pen and ynke,
floats down like cobweb scraps to settle
as dust upon an empty chair
from which a man in pain and drink
has clambered into air and gone
beyond the tall sash, eighteen-paned,
to friendly distances where hills,
no longer sooty, wake to welcome,
conjubilant, the dauntless boots
and anoraks of Albion.

XXVII

The organ heaves its direst rumble
while coughing and snot-noises die.

The choir attacks *Jerusalem*,
then struggles up a notch to raise
Warner whose immortal pen
as high as maybe, where poor Jigger,

on thermals of hyperbole
has reached the bright imaginary green
and found at last within the dazzle
his shape and size of place exactly.

XXVIII

Voices disperse, and choristers
attempt their lives without rehearsal.

Above their heads, the organist
deserts his nest and switches off
the light that lit the keys and stops.

Desks slam like shots, a muffled fart
moves on the day like any other.

XXIX

Half-mast, a fresher St George banner shifts
as mist warms in the Masters' Garden
and thins to snake-trails on the playing fields.

Whenas the ecstacy has end, the skies
within this future we are making
unclasp the ground while Albion
hugs closer what her myths disguise.

XXX

The sweet o' the year is rising up
so dewy and so odorous
from out of England's snowy orchards,

to scent the isle, all lands excelling,
where Jigger has inherited
his long dream of her heights and woods,
and freedom of her unmapped meadows

Fuimus Troes!

Fag-ash and whisky glass survive
a dwindling moment as he slips
the minds of feckless sons of Brutus.

Their clownish shapes a coined show,
the poore schoolmasters weep,
schoolmasters weep and they are woe,
and then do silence keep.

Yet soldier on, thou frumious Trojans,
turn blackboards into cliffs of chalk
in those true-blue academies
from which no Englishman retires, wherein
no women and no scarecrows dwell,
and skirmish joyfully with silly boys
like Blake, and Shakespeare, and Purcell.

FROM

The Glass Swarm

(2008)

Sir Entrepreneur

Between the workers and the wealth is strife
in regions perilous to honest men,
where goblins chuckle and the marsh fire burns.
Your brave steed trembles, and his eyes roll madly.

Put up your visor, and let me escort
you onward safely, for the light grows dim
and soon the path breaks, as it drops
in zigzags through enchanted hangers

where roots rear up, and watchful stones
lie bedded under quilts of moss.
We shall discover, while the day still lingers,
an elfin briefcase in the queachy ferns

and in it costings you have need of badly
to smooth the feathers of your auditors,
the ravens and the hooded crows.
You'll be their breakfast if you show a loss.

Those creaks we hear are limb on limb
as dead trees clutch their living kin,
like bankrupts and their creditors,
pulled down by ivy on the muddy slopes.

Your shield is smirched. Your plume hangs sadly.
Lord may I say, with your permission,
my castle stands a bow-shot hence.
Five hundred businessmen are there, each one

at wine beside his lady wife
in merry conclave and good countenance,
and if your errand may be deemed the sort
to turn a profit, they will fund you gladly.

The Naturalist

The Reverend Collingwood Pringle writes to his son, 1862

Inland we have another burning day,
but you, I trust, are cooler by the sea
in that calm haven, out of reach,
while your fine fads and theories bedevil
the task of men who preach revealed religion.
Wild roses are now done, but here and there
a field of uncut grass contains
spikes of sorrel, standing to attention
among the moon-faced dog-daisies
you'd call *chrysanthemum leucanthemums.*
Beside our stream, the green-scaled dragonflies
are plentiful and heavy on the air,
with small ones too, you will remember,
like fragile tubes of blue, winged glass.
You see, I'm quite the naturalist.

I wonder if, when one decides to free
oneself from something – duty, or a place –
you've noticed that a pause occurs
sufficient to allow the future
to squeeze into a smaller space?
Sometimes, I think, such pauses last forever.
I'm sleepy, and imagine only
the dull façade of that hotel – your face
inclined towards your specimens
and notebooks, on a balcony
reflected by a sea-slicked beach
the bogus progress of the waves leaves level –
and every day no letter comes.
Meanwhile, this five-pound note and scribble travel
with love from one no longer young, or clever.

The Silver of the Mirror

In time his expences brought clamours about him, that overpowered the lamb's bleat and the linnet's song; and the groves were haunted by beings very different from fawns and fairies.

SAMUEL JOHNSON, *Lives of the English Poets,* 'Shenstone'

As if reflected by the street, the soil
he stands on, with his long nose raised
to sniff the nearness of the revolution,
accepts the clean blade of his hoe
and scatters slowly, as through antique glass.
It is a matter of above, below.
He wears knee-breeches and a tricorn hat,
and mumbles verse into his plain jabot
of which he is the pleased but modest author.
His mild voice coaxes lawns and trees
to ripple through translucent tarmac,
still carrying the sentiments
he adds to them, on painted plaques,
of Thoughtfulness, of Sadness, and of Pity.
We tear the pavements up to reach his garden
and roar like beasts in pain, as boundaries break,
to find ourselves reduced by what we spoil.

And yet we are his comrades, and our horror
an upside-down ideal while, hoof to toe,
we struggle to assist him as we churn
parterres to mud and trample flat
the topiary and pergolas
he has maintained are beautiful, and wreck
the patterned walks, the symmetries
he laid out to reflect unchanging order.
The dream is his, and ours the revelation
that animates all malcontents.
The rumpus of our anguish fills the city.

Meanwhile, within the silver of the mirror,
beyond the ruined portico
and fountains with their splendours mired to wallow,
the cornfields and the hills where flocks are grazed
are as his verses promise, yet more golden,
and at his feet the seeds of terror grow.

The Squirrel

Not yet, perhaps not here, but in the end,
And somewhere like this.

PHILIP LARKIN

You talk to sunshine on the photograph
that blears our unremembered faces
and mirrors yours, within a thin black frame.
Your flowers are very cheerful in their vases.
We did not wish you to be put in here,
or see your footprints, as you drag your shins
beneath a floral dressing-gown
across the mop-slicks in the corridor.

Here's where you dream you tripped a snare
that closed forever on a whiff
of disinfectant, and a pain that lingers.
You're like the squirrel on the chandelier,
we try to reach you, but our fingers
grasp only air, and up you go,
beyond our help, to where your name
comes vacantly from far below.

You planned to age like poetry:
lyric and elegy becoming one
in celebration of the verb *to be.*
To kiss you, we blot out the sun.
We did not wish you to be made of stuff
morphine can manage till your smile begins
to claim that dying is the same
as painless waking, and no damage done.

Quince Blossom

There is no air, each leaf that falls
does so from lassitude, while you push on
through rhododendrons, unkempt quinces.
Why should we mock your axiom
that wishes, forged by settled wills,
are facts that alter circumstances,
or doubt your clever stratagem
to get back somehow to the lawn,
the tilting sundial and the rusty pram,
where lank grass snags your weary toes?
We don't call what you did a sin,
and no one any more knows what you've done
except the two of us, inside your head.
Approach the house. Break down the door.
The only room has furniture
too heavy for the floor, and walls
not quite the colour of your skin:
quince blossom, maybe, or the one
like lamp-light shining through your mother's ear,
as she bends down to kiss your nose
and leave you happy in your little bed
for one last time before she goes.

The Pickle Tub

There's still no water in the lake.
And then this morning when the sun
arrived between the shutter bars,
it burned my best arm, as I stretched
to let it in, but couldn't reach.
I rang, for all the good it did,
and called, but no one heard me calling.
Poor Daddy had his laces sponged and pressed
each time his shoes were cleaned, his pocket linings
unstitched and laundered every week.
The wood we used to picnic in
when we were girls – and so alike –
that hangs on one side of the hill
above the flooded pumping house,
is now a forest, in which good and evil
giants find and lose each other, brawling.
Go there and join them, I suggest,
and don't come back. I've had enough.
It's obvious that since you died
this pickle tub expands until
tomorrow's bigger, but seems farther off,
and every day speeds up the sense of falling.

Danse Macabre

Let's wish the porcelain goodnight, its sleep
unbroken in its cabinet,

and sweet dreams to the Canaletto
of sunlight on a campanile,

obscured by shadows in this swirling room,
adjusting triangles in peace, while steely

ripples widen on smoke-darkened water.
Goodnight to niches in which lilies weep.

Each guest has pleased his opposite:
Uncouthness and Dishevelment

have danced with Ease and Dignity
across the yielding, talc-strewn floor,

Youth has pranced with Age, and Body
has re-engaged with Soul, to tunes

no longer heard, which all the skills
of living orchestras can merely echo.

The black-clad servants are somnambulant.
From off the gallery drop pale balloons

to lift abruptly, as a door
swings open elsewhere, and the draught is sweet.

It's nearly time for rest. The hills
are shedding darkness from their stature

beyond the graveyard, and light saps the gloom
where candles splutter while we sit

in dancing-pumps of dust and draw
cobwebs around us on the window-seat.

Cuneiform

These cold walls have been papered with a murder
of crows among grey foliage
but half-obliterated once
in thin emulsion, and the floorboards spattered
as if with guano under dust.
The great desk must have come in through the window
that also lets in moonlight, on a book
forever open, an abandoned page –
the secret of the only code worth cracking –
hand-lettered, as with wedge-shaped splinters.
You would be thrilled to read the curse
in good plain English on the back
that condemns all who meddle in such matters
to be devoured by need to know.

A lidless eye has overlaid the moon.
Be very careful on the creaking
stairs and landing. Where's that ounce
of sense to tell you not to trust
the feeling that, for you, the eye is winking?
When you doss down inside a green cocoon
of sleeping-bag, your tape-recorder
will pick up interrogatory croaking
while still switched off and not in working order.
Outside are prints of crows' feet in the snow
of human size, but you are shrinking
to be pursued through folios of winters
and not wake up to hear the window shattered
or bare your pale skin to an inky beak.

The Redesdale Rowan

From now on I will be dispensing
with ramblers' maps, and all desire
to find the flora of this rabbit-lawn
listed in my guidebook to the fells,
or read the secret of the storm-shot rowan –
that should have fallen, yet has berries dancing
blood-red on leafy carousels –
in some botanical grimoire.
The day is warm. My feet are aching.
It is too late, with sunshine in my eyes,
to care which insect air force is commencing
a mass-attack of lullabies.
I shall approach the tree and dream there, waking
to hang my branches with a peal of bells.

The Lens

Your look is wide-eyed and direct,
while I have puckered eyelids, and my head
between my thumbs to point the lens
and frame your fine-boned fidgeting.
But now it's you that's focused, as you lean
towards the window to inspect
a small boy, busy in the lane,
who is the child we never had
although we prayed each time we fucked.
He has a roving glance, a stone to fling,
and juggles with a nifty flick
beneath his leg, as if to prove
insouciance, then aims with love
straight for the glass but hits the brick.

The Parting

The out-by in the corner of our worst,
most useless pasture has his look.
It is so steep the stones fall loose
beneath your boots and keep on falling.
He couldn't do a hand's turn without groaning,
and now he's in the newspaper for quoting
in books about the working folk.
See how his letters gather dust
as time goes on, behind the clock, unopened.
The track up there has worn deep, like the parting
he dug into his hair with soap
for lack of Brylcreem, on that sunny morning
he took our money from the cocoa-tin,
and left before his conscience woke.

Sea Fever

Why not come out again and kick my head
till it resumes identity
as half a lobster pot? Unwrap my skin
of polythene from driftwood, weeds and stones?
You'll find my fingers have acquired extensions
that comb the pleats of sea and gather
the stuff I need to build another body,
this time for you, my twin, my lover,
of buoyant and appalling beauty.
Your darkening footprints on the wet sand shrink
to dimples and your hotel bed
feels the tide shift and begins to sink
while I am downstairs at the desk already,
insistant, and the worse for drink.

The Tourist

The tourist at this moment will not stir
but stares beyond the cypresses
towards unmelted snow on sharp sierras
as if his eyes were new again.
A girl is sweeping, hushing an old broom,
and speaks politely but he will not answer.
He finds the scents of myrtle and of jasmine
insufficient, like the dark pinetum
and all the thread-like veins of lichen.
Tell him the colour of the crumbling tower
is not valerian, yet not quite rose.
He has remembered a young dancer.
Above the lizard on the broken column
he sees the trembling of the stars.

Après-midi

On the jetty is a grey collection
of packing-cases, a piano,
a limp flag hanging from a crooked staff,
the navigation office, closed.
This is a good day for the turtle,
the sand-caked boy who finds a starfish,
the tethered cockerel, beneath a tree
fantastical in swags of moss.
Upstream, mud-banks are volatile
and teem with crocodiles. The river's low.
Our progress will not thereby be affected.
Inside the Residence, a dusty echo
returns the laughter of a large pink lady
who wants to take her clothes off and be fiction.

St George's Day

For centuries the same sun has been sinking
here, where we loiter to invoke
the green, embroidered by long-fingered shadows
of branches coming into leaf, the drumming
and piping over, and the people –
who danced today and work the land in common –
cupping hands into the cool mill-brook,
which are our own hands, but with callouses.
Beside the inn door, at a solid table,
a ballad-seller, and two dairy-women,
sing the language we are thinking.
As Hob the landlord gobs for luck
into their ale, and picks his nose,
new worlds grow outward from the sunlit oak.

Black Country Browning

Here's where the forges were, the crucible
where we fought fire and smoke and sin
to cast a fancy from a flower-bell,
or catch a sunset-touch in glass
for chapel windows that began to glow
as far as the antipodes.
We coupled on the warm stone by the furnace,
which brings us down to thee, grown up so well
without our piety or taste in verse.
We burnished hammers with our skin,
but it consoles us that our bishops knew
of chorus-endings from Euripides,
as we sink deeper where the anvils rust
into the centre of the compass-rose.

FOLLY WOOD

All haile the noble Companie,
Students in holy Alchimie,
Whose noble practice doth them teach
To vaile it with a mistie speech.

The Hunting of the Greene Lyon

Fermentation

The night is creeping up behind the day
and all our keys are searching for their locks.
To be misled about the greater good,
and botch the things we're meant to do,
is blameless as the rot between your teeth.
The whisky on your breath would fell an ox.
Come back with me across the muddy fields
to drink another at the *ferme ornée*
and watch the moon rise at my study window,
bewitchingly from Folly Wood.
I'll teach you how to hold it at the zenith
between your thumbs, until it yields
to gentle pressure and stops all the clocks.

Sublimation

Leave us this morning if you wish, but first
spare time to meet our floating harp.
Please make sure that the door is shut,
then call her gently and observe
how groans of vanished poets lift her up,
and birdsong from long-silent beaks
resounds to make her tilt and quiver.
On rainy days, when Malkin is morose,
the harp will sometimes stamp her foot
upon the parquet, and make starlings burst
like soot bombs from the hearth and box
his ears with black arpeggios.

Congelation

To find our whereabouts, look at the palm
of your left hand – the *thenar eminence*,
since we are scientific men – yes, yes,
or Mount of Venus if you wish, and see
an old stone farmhouse with embellishments –
a turret and a little park,
my study window with four branching lancets –
all taking shape beneath the sun
while you and I consult your fate together.
Be patient as the landscape gathers
about you in its own good time and weather.
The temple on the *hypothenar* knoll –
towards the South – my own Mount Cyllene –
pertains to Mercury, Hermes, or Thoth
in all his guises. To the North,
young Goldilocks, the green of thumb,
is Ceres, in the kitchen garden
levelled from the hill behind the house.
See how she skittishly unseats
potatoes for our casserole,
and throws aside her garments as she goes.
The roof, too, is of slabs of stone
between which blown seeds find an anchorage
as you have done, now look again
and pick us out among the terms and statues
that make this terrace quite a pantheon.
You will see further, when you find the courage.
A gleam of water, linking head and heart,
bisects your *palmar excavation* –
we are still scientific men –
through working meadows where a path ascends
along the Line of Destiny
to Folly Wood, the hanging dark
that cloaks the hillside at your fingers' ends.

Exaltation

When I'm despondent, Malkin makes me laugh
by reading with that squawk of his
adjusted to a boyish chime
and funnelled lips, as if to blow
or suck the letters off the page and leave
upon his lap not book but album.
Perhaps his face-parts are becoming stiff.
Tonight, if there are stars they will be fierce
and coat my Gothick bridge with rime,
the path as well, up which he'll go –
cold clockwork hungry for the taste of life –
if I provoke him and then set him off.

Conjunction

She is my keenest sharpener of knives,
and skilful with the apparatus
that traps the essence of the strong night air
which is assisting my rejuvenation.
A man is noble when he strives
to garner wisdom and to master nature
and true philosophers should not take wives.
Of course, propinquity and pulchritude
will not be overlooked, and thus
Miss Goldilocks has learned to please and tease.
When my indulgence prompts ingratitude,
she takes to girlish fits of rustication
and then my fond heart leaps to see her gain
the lawn and fields beyond the pantheon –
those absurd deities of my domain
extending limbs of mossy stone
as if to halt her by gesticulation –
then ford the trout stream on her hands and knees,

as naked as a naiad in the flood,
and climb an oak before my pack arrives
to tree her there till I am understood.

Cibation

This evening we shall make your finger bleed
to tempt those pretty singers from their nests,
that thrive on blood up by the temple,
and only blood, except a little pepper
which I provide to make them sing more purely.
You will enjoy their soothing anapæsts
the more so should our harp, as if she dreamt
their singing, let the darkling breeze
move among her strings and make them tremble
sufficiently to harmonise.
Be careful when they start to feed.
You'll see them take a very dove-like supper
unless the pepper makes them sneeze,
in which case they may change their ways entirely
and every eager beak become a blade.

Separation

The past is something a wise man discards,
but there are episodes to mention.
Since I grew up apart from other boys,
the victims of my first success with words
were lovers on a Davenport tureen.
They lived in gardens quite like mine
but less austere, you understand,
with ruined arches and tall banks of flowers
that leaned towards them on the porcelain
as he inclined, with half-closed eyes,

to doff his hat and kiss her hand
while she would tilt her fan in condescension.
I shrank myself so I could creep unseen
through roses, or behind an urn,
and ridicule the passing of their hours
beneath the glaze, until the joys
they longed for broke, in pale blue shards,
and scattered on the steps down to the lawn.

Multiplication

Correspondences reveal to natures
having the wit to read them, or the luck,
that highest knowledge is armillary
in its unfolding, known and knower
revolving, loop through loop and arc through arc,
about the limbs of God. Oh dear,
that clatter from the scullery –
my hip-bath knocked down from its hook –
means you-know-who is off again
on one more of her mad adventures. Look
how late blue twilight turns the stone
of pavement, balustrade, and pantheon,
to pewter, like your whisky flask,
which as you lift it shows the moon
her dull reflection. Pass it over.
That's better. Now let's stroll the lawn
between the trees – those mute philosophers,
who are like us both seed and sower –
and see how my ancillary
makes zigzag progress through the park,
a skinny flicker in the dusk
pursued by coiling, tumbling creatures
that breathe in daylight and exhale the dark
and are her mind's corollary.

Projection

Please open my four lancet windows wide
and sit beside me, in the musky air,
facing inward to my room and books
between the pale sky and the bare
three-cornered table, by the shadow-flecked
cheval-glass with carved vine leaves on its frame
and birds that, in the firelight, twitch their wings.
Drink up. It's not formaldehyde.
Tomorrow, you and I shall recommence
our studies and have done with logic chopping
or theory without effect,
and seek for knowledge fertile in performance.
Ignore poor Malkin, and the hiccuping
he makes to mock us as we charge our glasses
and all those disapproving looks
from she who tends the hearth for us, unswathed.
Such nothings in the shape of things
are unimportant, though they have their uses.
The night I fetched you here and had you bathed
and put up with your petulance,
you'd more than had your share of whisky supping.
Well done. Chin Chin. I'm glad you came
and took hold of the moon with such assurance.
Things are since then, I trust, a little clearer.
The man you thought you were must be rebuked
in solemn sentences then stand aside
while what you are becoming is invoked
and enters – as your old life passes
before us in the bleary mirror –
as scorching brightness, and each gilt bird sings.

Solution

This morning light lacks strength. No doubt
the copper magus with his staff and cape
upon the weather-vane has turned about
to indicate an unpropitious quarter.
Close watching through the doleful hours
will inculcate contempt for rest
and strengthen your elastic powers.
Our privilege is work, advancing
philosophy towards the dark
of which the edge of brightness is a trap
we shall avoid, now we can trace
the root of tinctures to a dormant spark.
Do not be eager for success. Today,
we may not hope to boil the fire in water.
Try once again to give your thoughts a shape.
Twelve circling cherubim with lettered wings
about their shoulders, might we say,
and Arts and Sciences to sing and clap?
When Goldilocks brings porridge in at last
greet her politely, I suggest,
but turn your eyes from her beguiling body
and let your thoughts continue dancing
the Great Word with their feathered arms unfurled.
The daft girl has a pretty face,
but such allurements, and the scran she brings,
are merely echoes of a world
through which we have already passed.

Calcination

I watched you through binoculars
pick small stones in a daze and grip them hard –
as if in obscure shame for ease
or guilty pleasure in your circumstances –
then toss them into incense smoke
for Hermes, at his temple on the rise.
Well, since such mischief has been done,
we must be bold philosophers
and learn composure from the wise
not lose our heads like womenfolk.
If you were faithful to the ordinances –
correct but not meticulous –
the ritual may yet evoke
an Entity disposed to hurt you less
than these same pebbles, if I squeeze
your hand. Like that! Be on your guard.
Rules have been broken by today's endeavours.
Those stones are shifty as your eyes upon
the table, as I rearrange their glances.

Putrefaction

Tell me again about that twilit pause
in which the trees – if trees they were –
with all the thickets of the world implicit,
closed ranks about you, with each trembling twig
alert for answers from the air
that blanched your breath, and numbed your fingers
against the pewter of the whisky flask
and darkened as you took a swig.
Then how abruptly the engulfing road –
as you expanded on your choice
to quit the treadmill for the whirligig –
detached itself from destination,
an attribute of which no trace now lingers.
In that I was myself of course complicit
through true philanthropy, which knows no vice.
Meanwhile, remember why the toad
devours the eagle and the lion –
all but their crowns of leaf-green fire –
then sleeps until his loathsome sores
are jewels on a perfect skin.
I must enable this. Your task
will be to praise him when he wakes,
as we shall, into paradise.
Unlatch your tongue and then rejoice.
They are in each of us, the thin
dissecting cry a baby makes,
the soothing remnant of a deeper voice.

Recapitulation

Today we walk through fire, not air,
and you shall weave a wife or daughter
to leave behind in Folly Wood
as soon as we have done with reaping,
and all our work will be a dream
that once trod on your face, and stumbles
away into a nodding head
of gleanings bound with baler twine.
The space between us is becoming flame
as clouds that harden into lead
intensify the afterglow.
This lough has not been fed by any stream
but by the dripping conifers
where we shall hang your dolly knot –
a noddle like a harp, that trembles
to wind and birdsong – gently tapping
the cross-branch of a pine. You know her name
because you loved her long ago
and would forget her, if you could.
The meadows are incarnadine
about the *ferme ornée*, no trespassers
disturb a prospect that resembles
a palm unclenched – a window shut
on purpose to continue peeping –
as light like gold moves off the cooling water.
The dusk is warm, the stars benign,
and you have nothing to return to there
where what you were is in my keeping.

The Brass Band

Oh that I had given up the ghost, and no eye had seen me!
Job 10: 18

You claimed this view could soothe you with its sermon
of wildness tamed
and turned to English parkland, nearer heaven
than you were, choking with the cough, ashamed
because Jerusalem remained unbuilt
in spite of all you'd done. The nursery clock
would hiccup by your bed again so merrily!
I'd dream you rode a rocking horse full tilt
home down the years, your white unbloodied smock
embroidered freshly in my memory.

You'd find such eloquence to speak of vice
and poverty.
I'd have your sisters read your letters twice
and total up the times, as we took tea,
you'd mention rickets, say, or sewage farms
and then we'd smile together as we'd try
to picture your excursions, primed with prayer,
your tracts and Bibles dragging down your arms,
about those labyrinths where industry
disorders nature and befouls the air.

Be still. Although I hardly see at all,
it hurts my eyes
each time you fidget with the parasol.
The sun to me is that with which you'd rise
each day with ardour for the public good,
a disc obscured by smoke, deprived of rays
by all the furnaces of busy hell.
Sit back and gaze towards the hanging wood
above the temple by the lake, the maze
you used to say you'd solve when you were well.

It's said by men who have the landscape eye
that concave ground
will ever be the source of tranquil beauty,
which same configuration draws forth sound.
Go now, as flower beds invade the lawns
and brass glints from a birdcage made of iron.
The new age has produced, in its confusion,
a kind of orchestra of artisans
who own their instruments and wives in common.
Their music is the fruit of your compassion.

The Cockatrice

No smoke is rising from the warm brick chimneys
towards a blue sky, without meaning,
where emptiness and light compete.
Please put your book down on the grass
and make your face a real sunbather's face.
Now conjure up a cock and hen,
horse-size, and harnessed to a cage of iron
on slow wheels, with an egg in it,
alive and massive but as cold as ice.

Your mother won't say who your father was.
So call to her, where she is leaning
against the rail of the verandah
to tease a playful shadow. Call again,
until she turns and shades her eyes
in sudden love and then comes running,
the shadow dancing at her feet,
to greet the hatchling and unbolt the door
and be the first snack that your dream will eat.

The Acorn

I love him, but I cannot like him; and as for taking his arm,
I should as soon think of taking the arm of a tree.

A friend writing about Henry Thoreau

Chainsaws have been slicing trees in half
all day where paths are soft and there are falls
of loose earth from the unsafe banks.

Their yelps disturb the potted fern
beside his window, as autumnal air
becomes more pungent and the breeze

resounds like bad news in the wire
but does not wake the telephone.
The world has put up with his harmlessness

among these pictures, books, and cases
of *objets trouvés* from his lonely strolls
for long enough, and that malaise

that keeps him self-sufficient and well-meaning.
The lambs are restless on the hill, a calf
takes fright in its familiar haining

as gravity weighs down his walls
as if to bed the man in stone. Death wears
a smile cut into bark and knows

how weakly sap flows up his shanks,
and also in which chest of drawers
upstairs, beneath his socks, an acorn grows.

The Green Corn

Now we're done and harvested, remember us
grinding the bugbear of the bourgeoisie –
repulsive, squirming, and ridiculous –
beneath our marching boots. The century
caught fire and edged our shadows with a nimbus
that spooked the pale ghost of uncertainty
as new dawns broke, and kerchiefed girls went swinging
their strong limbs to the rhythm of our singing.

We learned in cinemas to love the murder
of cartoon characters, and came to find
that squeamishness is soluble in laughter.
Our revolution was a sleep of mind,
to build the dream that reasserts the order
which progress must impose on humankind.
But soon the dream in turn informed the will
and we found breathing enemies to kill.

How pinkly then our shirts and dirndls shone
as earth soaked up the colours of our banner,
and children carried grief and shattered bone –
the Jew's nose, top hat, and the big cigar –
to tinkling music from a gramophone
in gratitude as trophies to our leader –
moustached and dapper in his dungarees –
while we like green corn rippled round his knees.

Recessional

There go the victims of the winter weather
on that bleak crown of stubble land,
more thoughtfully disposed by far
than when they used the calendar
to wipe their arses. Hand in hand,
they jigged and twirled through spring together,
dancing the hornpipe of the blood,
and drunk they blundered in a summer wood.

But this is not what they imagined,
that fresh lives gather round them, pressing
closer to be claimed and lived
while who they were is thin stuff, sieved
by careless time from pools of guessing.
Their names are what daft rooks have penned
with flourishes on darkening air
and that exacerbates despair.

Although their progress has become unsteady
against the texture of black fields, the arc
of soundless and advancing ocean,
they're moving forward where a gate stands open
on all the paths they've still to walk
to where they always were, but ready
this time perhaps to find a sign
whenever memory and love combine.

The Ballroom at Blaxter Hall

We might be anywhere but are in one place only.
DEREK MAHON

Here is the home of lost romance,
where gilded chairs are stiffly paired,
each uppermost inverted, legs in air
to tent the dust-sheets, hammocking the dust.

The grand piano, like a catafalque
to house the still form of Despair,
is also sheeted, and attempts a groan.
The fireplace yawns. The afternoon

outside is always almost dusk,
and cocked like an enormous ear
to catch the whisper of a waterfall.
With only cobwebs to support its bulk,

a bagged and massive chandelier –
the wasps' nest of a glass-swarm – hangs prepared
to drop at once if you should call
for wine and roses, or the chance to dance.

The Stitchers

The consequence of poetry is shame.
DOUGLAS DUNN

What they're embroidering is us, full pelt
through clutching memory, clump after clump,
until each likeness stumbles, and its rump,
in artful needlework, yields to the grip

of grinning anthropophagi.
We're in a version of the Feast of Guilt,
where consequences eat intention,
chewing fingers, howking out an eye,

then relishing the succulence
of butchered limb and bloody stump.
They'll stitch us into grief until we die,
and yet the teeth that gnaw and rip

at silk or corpse meat are our own.
The only exit is impenitence,
or one small window in the word *goodbye*
through which we would be mad to jump.

Home Is the Sailor

The streets have jetsam underfoot, and haar
thins briefly to reveal a hanging clue
of light that means a door ajar.

A whatnot made of rickety bamboo
leans in the damp scent of the hall. Please rest
your head against it till it tilts askew

then stumble out, in skirts of mist.
A square of dirt where bins are kept,
becomes the Garden of the Blessed,

and opalescent gleams have crept
among the postcards in the window,
illuminating schoolgirl script

and *noms de lit*, with posies in the margin,
that spell the news that paradise
docks in the haven of the here and now,

while such as we are spume that flies
from nature's solving and dissolving surge,
which rolls beneath us as we rise

to fall back on the deep and merge
where fog-horns grunt, and ships diverge.

Greta

The Hon Gertrude Pringle returns to Blaxter Hall, 1939

The factory succeeds the family, and gentry
means nothing now. The day enlarges
dwindling pastures into boulder country

along the thin road lined with mountain ashes
where, as a girl, I dreamed of hovering
above the one-street villages

and tenants in them, who seemed smoothly working
models of themselves. Now Europe is at war
to spoil the fun I had discovering

the gymnast and her furniture
inside my head, between Berlin and Paris,
far from this wilderness of useless moor

to which I'll bring a squad of men and lorries
with steel and glass to build the new aesthetic
and smash my father's pile of worries,

despite the finest plasterwork
in all Northumberland. Here is the bridge,
then more expensive husbandry. An oak

leaps up to greet me by the gothick lodge,
and here come Armstrong and his missus,
who drink, and live on neaps and cabbage,

and will not defamiliarise
their objectives. That kind of *dreck* ignores
the hygiene of the optical, denies

modernity its necessary laws.
More jolting, then manoeuvres to perform,
and – *Scheiße* – I'm backwards in a room outdoors

lit brightly, but by no means warm,
that has a light breeze with a little moan
and monsters, signalling. I think the problem

this epoch faces is its situation
here on this lawn. *Salut.* My name is Greta,
inventor of the ergonomic kitchen,

ambassadress of function and of beauty,
perfectibility, in sisterhood,
of social structures, human spirit,

and purity of race and blood.
Don't drop me. Don't let my hair unravel.
My skirt must not at any time touch mud.

I loathe this damp path between banks of laurel
which tunnelling vermin undermine.
But there's a shimmer on the mossy gravel

like thought becoming crystalline
beside the Seine, the Spree, the Tyne.

The Ventriloquist and the Wooden Girl

Although we were the one act in the show
to match the equinoctial gales,
our audience left early in the rain

the better to continue drinking,
and spend the whole night breaking bottles
then beating glass into the willow trees

in order to revive these shrinking days,
encouraged by the scarecrows of the village
who own a copy of *The Golden Bough*.

But we have you, of course, there in the glow
beneath the exit sign. Step up on stage,
and don't be bashful while I teach you how

to pull the string that clicks her lips
into a kiss, and wrap her heels
efficiently behind your shins. She grips

more tightly when her varnished knees
vibrate to distant hammer-taps. Her eyes
reflect your future without blinking.

This is the last chance, as I'm sure you know,
to get the measure of the ullage
your skull contains, and find your brain,

and hear the wooden girl herself explain,
with eructations and resounding glottals,
the quick way to prevent the sun from sinking.

Wentletraps

After an unwritten story by Anton Chekhov

Cupboards are locked along the corridor
that stinks of overcoats, a violin
has scraped its notes together in an attic,

and now all's still but for these rigmaroles
about his plan to plant our bodies
like seed potatoes in the soil of Russia

and grow our souls in peace on some estate
he needs my money to afford.
Outside, the drenched back of the storm has bent

to let the moon shine on his furniture
and boxes stacked where gravel meets the lawn.
His wife snores lightly in his aunt's old seat

beneath the icon, and his servants
sleep in the shelter of the gooseberries.
My own view is that soul grows as the brain

is fed by thought, and by chromatic
light but recently observed, to wit
the faint flash darting from a marigold

or else from monk's-hood or from indian-pinks
at sunset in a summer of dry weather.
That electricity controls

this process has been made apparent
by Haggern in St Petersburg. I'm bored.
How broad his nose is as he smirks and winks!

In times of strife, it's true, our native mould
becomes the bed for which a brave man looks.
Meanwhile, to have done with this fool's palaver

I'd join the troglodytes who live in holes
like book-lined wentletraps, the cleverest
residing in the deepest, with more books.

The Bather

We must be careful with this memory:
the context is already shaking loose
in which we all drift back as if we're sorry.

A younger dog behind the house
rehearses a remembered bark
of ownership to welcome us

together with a fresh gust from the loch
that shifts your papers in the escritoire
and worries leaves along the chestnut walk.

The keyhole of the rosewood drawer
admits light to a corner of the letter
you wrote to tell the world you didn't care.

That gillie in his shirt-sleeves knew no better
than tug his forelock by the path you took
thirty years ago, down to the water.

Let's hang your legend on its hook
beside our coats in your cold kitchen
and drink your whisky in the ingle-nook.

You weren't a bad girl, on reflection,
and there are worse ways to pretend to die
than leave your night-dress to attract attention,

your towel on a tree to dry,
and live the life of Riley, then goodbye.

Snow at Fourlawshill Top

The silence that, for mischief, loves
night screech, fox cry, lonely weeping,
welcomes this cold whisper blowing
residuum, like shallowing
impressions of a nib that moves
to shape a word but leaves the page
a brighter blank, the thought unspelt
that makes the after-image of each pang
of headlights half a mile along
the road to Buteland in the shot white dark
a memory of less and less.

And even less and less will dimple, seeping
to honeycomb, a crust of melt
for Wansbeck, Coquet, and the Aln,
retreating to uncover grass
and blunt, assertive daffodils.
So let the unicorns of blizzard rage
about their business on the Wanney Hills
and write a big word with their icy hooves
that means my garden and returning lawn,
where light and memory can strike a spark
from crocuses like broken glass.

FROM

The Game of Bear

(2011)

The Tower

Deep in the masonry the gasps and hushes
of soot-falls visiting the hearths below
sound like a restless audience.
Meanwhile my lady sighs and adds a hiss
and more mist to the mist that lifts
the pele above a curtilage
all evidence for which dissolves in guesses.
She is the loveliest of chatelaines
and coldest, as the water freezes
in mossy cisterns and our blood
if it still ran would curdle. There's a plaid
to snuggle into on the window-seat
but she eschews it as she leans
far out and yearningly above a fleet
of tree-tops severed from their trunks that drifts
and sinks beneath her breath towards the Rede,
a river well known for its greed in flood
and then when trods are dry for thieves
and Scotsmen. Her chill privilege
like mine – her walled-up rival – is to know
how being beautiful and dead addresses
the exigency of aesthetic sense
and how devotedly our sweet
admirer on the stream's far bank reclines
repining by the boundary stone of this
and every earthly parish, among bushes
worse than bears, and waits for kisses
beneath a counterpane of fallen leaves
from which adhesive camouflage
his skull emerges then his bony feet
as thunder mutters and the lit mist fizzes.

The Empress

In summer at her palace by the dunes
the sand blows in among the adjectives
we reach for to describe our happiness
on postcards scribbled to the wind and sun.
The light each evening is compressed
not quite to darkness by the shortening nights
and soon the dawn discovers us in bliss.
Like fools before us and fools yet unborn
we work unflaggingly at her command,
patching the roof, or side by side
uprooting docks and dandelions
or mending pot-holes on her tennis lawn
in sand-squalls, raking, shaking sieves,
while she strings nets with paper kites
to charm us and preserve the seed
she scatters with a lengthening hand
from birds that have the looks of lost companions.
She brings us cold herb omelettes, with olives
we dip in red wine to wash off the sand
that clings to them and covers us.

Gustav Mahler Returns to Maiernigg

Ferrier sings the *Kindertotenlieder*
and in a pause for breath he's up and clears
the hedge that shelters three sides of the stone
at Grinzing where they lowered him in silence
he did not wish to hear disturbed. He'll snap
his legs out from the hollows of his knees
and choose the quickest route. Increasing pace
his head leans forward following his chin
and he maintains a pounding step
along the fast lanes of the autobahns
to towns and villages with balconies
of flowers and sausages and pushes hard
through fields of maize where pylons tuck
their feet in shrubbery the plough can't reach.
His forest welcomes him. It is a breeder
of transformations and perceives
that he might be a tree a bit like Bogarde
cast in the Doomed Composer role,
a birch perhaps, grown tangled at the crown
but looking dapper in its bark. The leaves
that fall among his fingers are not tears.
Pines launch themselves in ecstasies
towards the narrow sky. His toes seek water.
Ferrier's voice extends again.
The pause that fetched him home was far too brief
to trade a grand piano for the space
in which to make a playground by the beach
for Putzi with a lattice fence, her father
there to notice her. No time to stack
and burn the works of Kant and Bach and Goethe.
Behind his steel-rimmed glasses there's a face
where lichen thrives and caterpillars crawl
across a mind that feels no grief
but knows the price of music was his daughter.

Unity in the Englischer Garten

She went to Parteitagen as to Mass
and still prays to the Führer, but in vain.
She let the dear storms commandeer a flat
on Agnesstrasse. When the Jews who own
nothing now but old age and their bags had gone
she turned her future in the lock.
She dreams that lava-heaps and cinder-cones
rise from hot sand when she tries to run
and then veiled women in a great black car
as dawn comes crush her in a Swinbrook lane.
Now rooks with silver swastikas convene
mock parliaments among the trees
beside the Haus der Kunst. The day is warm
and she is beautiful. She sees
across the park the Isar fuss
among its channels in an English manner
with swarming khaki backwaters. Her brain
must calculate her worth. The world's at war.
The British consulate is off the phone.
There's no one left to play with or to shock.
A green bench shimmers in the sun.
Wearing her crimped hair like a hat
she sits there to relax and points the gun
against her blank cherubic face.
She is a kind of saint. We need not care
nor spare the time to think of her again.

The Claxon Case

She waits for ever for the dinner gong
and scans the shrubbery wherein the queenly
rhododendron and the kingly laurel,

like dancers who are also lovers, place
the leaf-tips of their lower limbs together
as if awaiting music that the pheasant –

named Mr Claxon – who still haunts the lawn –
as she does – will produce, not with his throat,
which is the dry bulb of a motor horn,

but by the elegance of his demeanour
which draws from evening air a melody
as sweet as poison on a sugar cube

dissolving as the years do on her tongue.
This strolling rajah, wattled to out-glare
the sunset, finds his sabre-tail

too cumbersome. He lifts a foot
as if he has no shoelace in his shoe –
in fact no shoe – and then a note

then silence then another note, a phrase
that takes the measure of his sloth-slow pace,
cuts through the gloaming solemnly

and distantly and thin, persistent
in answering its echo with the question
her fateful holiday was meant to settle.

Below his oily eye and Crippen collar,
he sports a waistcoat with the ochre glow
of warnings chalked beneath the seats of chairs –

and once behind her wardrobe door – obscenely
elaborating a suggestion
that impropriety could happen here

where Mrs Claxon keeps a small hotel
that has a zinc bath like a torpedo tube
which policemen come to look at, and to smell.

Fortitude

Fed up on lard in unpoliced wards
we breed laboriously and are extinguished
young and without publicity.
Untroubled by monotony and stench
our children play among the mournful doves,
half-skipping in the slimy yards
half-marching, keep uncertain step,
and laugh now clouds unload a vaporous drench
as we did when in better days we'd slip
to bathe in storm-drains of a dreaming city
of pastel-coloured boulevards,
broad piazzas, fountain-washed,
stern virtues and platonic loves.
We grunt and are appeased. Our fists unclench.

The Devil

O mad dog of the short June night
forsaking spouse of any race
at present on this earth have pity.
Don't violate the innocent tableau –
two-legged hound plus whelp and bitch –
at that uncurtained window, light
cast upward on each smiling face
from birthday candles, and the music low.
Don't even pause to scratch an itch
among the fireflies and night-scented stocks
but wedge a street map of the city
between your frothy jaws and tuck
your trousers in your socks and go
on all fours quickly to the world you know.

The Juggler

Spring's a girl in the streets at night.
EWAN MACCOLL

Biodegradeably, my winter hags
snort toxic back-draughts and kick up a storm
beside the road to you. They like the stink
and sub-stink of the underpass,
the low life of the salty verge.
I make them knickers out of plastic bags
and give them needles and warm condom mittens.
But soon your daughter will emerge
between tall gateposts among shadow patterns
of leaves that match the uniform
her posh school wears. You like to think
that she's too good for me. She helps the grass,
by walking over it, to grow.
She'll get her kit off when I ask her though.

The Good Child

Her life is getting blurry at the edges
and no grown-up it seems has understood
the urgent whisper of the sea
that creeps inland as she skips over bridges
spanning the streams that feed the estuary
which are augmented by a dripping sky.
Each night she takes the safe way home.
She is obedient. And now she stretches
as tall as possible to turn the key.
Wet rats rummage in the hedges
but soon she's in a passage then a room
with one hard chair to sit on being good
and waiting for the ones who never come
until the sea does and the churning mud.

Penny Dreadful

A blade along the dull hide of a strop
sounds like my breath. I've strength to crawl
up past the sleeping bells and drop
down heavily where dew sobs on the leads,
an English town below me like a map,
Victorian and safe. Folk in their beds
dream me above them and my arms are long.
My hands have grown less human and are red
enough to choke the dawn. It's time to stop
and hug the weathercock. I shall not fall
into the net of right and wrong
or bait my conscience like a trap.
This is the end of what is done and said.
I left her bedroom like a butcher's shop.

BOBBY BENDICK'S RIDE

When thou shalt come into the marriage chamber, thou shalt take the ashes of perfume, and lay upon them some of the heart and liver of the fish, and shalt make a smoke with it. And the devil shall smell it and flee away.

Tobit 6: 16-17

Shoes grip cobbles to a car-horn tucket.
Nine crocodiles, *monsieur le prêtre,*
are ancient monuments of France. Hearts trip
along a rank of drums. The precious luggage,
Christ, His Mother, and a silk-lined turtle shell,
is shouldered, staggering in air
against the weight of which a fan
stirs damp aromas of the *plat du jour*
traditionnel, peculiar
to this vicinity. Marmot perhaps.
Blood pudding possibly. Identity
is not presumed upon. Our rendezvous
shall be the foyer of La Belle Hôtesse.

A muckle beast wi' fowre guid legs
is Bobby Bendick's mare,
but Auld Nip loups on twa cleft hooves
an' follows Bobby far.

Sometimes in reading and in walking I arrive
as of a sudden at a place in part
familiar and yet not clearly known
and hear my footsteps die away
ahead of me. Uncommon heat
is tightening the strings of summer's
theorbo. The swift-winged choirs
are over Otterburn that are not birds
nor are they cherubim. They see us plod
or jig like pismires on the molehill earth
that trammels us. I now perceive
that by remaining fools we may prevail.
A thin voice stretches and is broken.

A muckle beast wi' twa guid lugs
is Bobby Bendick's mare,
but Nip whae wears baeth lugs an' horns
heors Bobby from afar.

What stirs the air? I know this floor
on which my shadow moves. The huntsman's leg
bends through a crutch below the knee.
He is composed of tesserae
no one has seen who knows his name
for seven hundred years. He draws his bow
and eyes the buck. Who is the last
one to forget? The fish. Fine pleasances
are hereabouts I studied in
of sweet grass in the shade bestowed by oaks
and chestnuts. *L'enfant Enric* himself was not
more comfortable in his *carapace*
than I in those days with my head in books.

> *A muckle beast wi' twa guid een*
> *is Bobby Bendick's mare,*
> *but Nip wi' een like spairkin' lamps*
> *spies Bobby from afar.*

I am a gentleman the Lord has made
uncommon apt to read and walk at once
provided only that my pace
be easy and be regular. Vile Azariah
is no man but a crocodile
in his duplicity. My Bible goes
with me most often and has gathered grass
between its leaves, and such a harvest
of hedgerow foliage withal
to mark those passages I have discovered
most like to veins of profitable ore
that it has now a rustick look
in colour earthen, a most precious clod.

> *A muckle tail to thresh the air*
> *has Bobby Bendick's mare,*
> *but Auld Nip's tail's a muckle flail*
> *tae thresh puir Bobby sore.*

What man would not delight, placed in a garden
to make a survey of its rich collections?
Would groves and grottoes and the artful
wilds of it, the patterned flowers
and open vistas not delight his soul?
How tempting it is then to envy
the all-contriving Genius and strive
by stealth to steal away His secret treasure.
But might the man yet find himself
drawn back towards the gate he entered by
to find that now there is no gate
and where he came by is a darker path?
The reader casts a shadow on the page.

A foal o' fair Northumberland
is Bobby Bendick's mare,
but Bobby gans awa' tae France
an' skules wi' Ezra theor.

Gargoyles like crocodiles weep kisses
upon Sophia's upturned face –
where she is letting down her hair and sings
her secret names while clambering
the nine rungs of the shadow of a ladder –
and kisses on the cheeks of cobblestones.
I see her lean unsteadily
towards the dish of strawberries
I set out on my window-sill.
The Lisles Burn is descending in its linns
to fishponds and a dovecote. Now her song
is silenced by the roaring flutter
that dusts me in my stride and passes over.

True-hairted an' a Christian steed
is Bobby Bendick's mare,
she'll kick hor stable door tae spelks
if Ezra passes neor.

Acquaint me with her words. Her strawberry lips.
A brazier glows. Today the path
where white dust alternates with tender spots
of coolness in which shadows linger
has led to Woodburn or Lescar
and some small industry about an engine
compact of beams and ropes upon a husting
that has a purpose I shall ascertain
by asking. I am a priest and shall be told.
The fish that bit away the foot
shall not be captured but another
filleted for gall and heart and liver
according to the scheme of Azariah.

A loyal an' a jealous steed
is Bobby Bendick's mare,
if wicked Ezra tries tae moont
betimes he's kicked awa'.

I'll hire a car and drive to Paradise
through lynchet-meadows. In a pool
while bathing an offensive-looking trout
will no doubt speak to me. I shall be kind.
Responding pleasantly I will suggest
that we are friends and I breathe water
as he does. *Charmant mais sans merci, c'est moi.*
Nine days I shall abide there to perfect
my holiday. I like the music
the torrent makes, the dewy grass,
the early mass of birds, the clouds
snared on the summits in a net of gold.
Monsieur, I spit upon the *plage*.

Beneath a bonny rowan tree
stands Bobby Bendick's mare,
but Ezra's i' the Ingram Pool
whilst Bobby droons him theor.

Sophia has unclothed herself in smoke
of fish guts and incense. La Belle Hôtesse
is shut down and demolished among ghosts
fading from Pau Hunt photographs, plus-fours
and golf-clubs by the bust of Bernadotte.
The left hand of a Cagot pressed to death
upon a husting *lentement*
pour bien décourager les sorcières
is got by Azariah in exchange
for English money. Great wings will beat me down.
My gown and bands, the cloth I wear
protect me. O Beelzebub
make haste to help me. Make me rich.

Ezra's stairk across the back
o' Bobby Bendick's mare.
He'll tak the road tae Blaxter Bog
an' dee nae mischief mair.

Perceive the world through its disguises.
A ruined church. A ruined priest
to celebrate the Mass for bats. Behold.
This is my parish and my duty.
Look about you, Azariah,
and see a swarm of helicopters drown
in blue air over Corsenside. Today
the wise and merciful Theanthropos
will lead us to the bank of Ingram Pool
and set before us stepping-stones
from which to plunge our crafty souls
again to bathe yet not be cleansed.
I see a blackness and a quivering cloud.

By Chairford Bridge an' Grindstone Sike
gans Bobby Bendick's mare,
for Bobby's boond for Wanney Byre
tae hide hissel' awa'.

Upon a rocking stepping-stone the urge
to stride becomes less marked, yet stride I must.
The golden days go by. The taxi
sinks on its springs. The finest shoe
I ever boned and polished is enshrined
in a broken jar of cassoulet.
What's all this luggage, Azariah,
the nine great crocodiles of France
migrating to the River Rede?
Their hellish jaws. Sometimes a slant of music,
perhaps the Small Pipes, or a known aroma,
or light upon the peaks accuses me.
I am a man whom Wisdom shall reward.

By Stiddlehill an' Hepple Heugh
gans Bobby Bendick's mare,
whilst Bobby's grippin' roond hor neck
an' greets wi' mairtal feor.

The sun each day when it declines
engraves such pictures with a fiery needle
my mind makes on the sweltering clouds
of owl-eyed lust and Azariah
the great fish in a black coat threshing water.
Each night I beat his head again with stones.
He drowned. Yet he returns. The room is empty.
Hark. She sounds. There's nothing there. I am content.
When Wisdom shall again climb through my window
she will converse with me alone.
Monsieur, there's time to take myself to France
and dig a deeper grave. The hand
that rests beside mine on the altar points.

A beast wi' teeth like kirkyaird stanes
is Bobby Bendick's mare,
but Auld Nip's like a crocodile
wi' Bobby in his maw.

Matins at nightfall. Evensong at dawn.
The roof of Cuddy's kirk is gone. Walls totter.
I'll burrow like a marmot at Wanney Byre
before the quick-nosed fiends, the dogs of hell
shall have my blood for pudding. Snares
there are in my resolve, snares in my doubt.
Horizons burn. Hark. The infernal Nimrod
sniffs me out. If God preserve me, let him roar!
Great wings beat down. Virtue decays. The earth
sings psalms to darkness in that quivering cloud
of endless pain and frantic mirth.
No one meddles here but me. The Cagot's hand
points true. My horse is swift. What stirs the air?

Nip i' the cleft ca'd Wanney Byre
spares Bobby Bendick's mare,
but hales puir Bobby deun tae hell
wi' Ezra ivor mair.

Artemis Before a Prospect of Blaxter Hall

Oil on panel, circa 1800. Artist unknown.

The elongated steeplechaser arches
her neck sufficiently to tug a groom
in gaiters to his toes. She wears her plucky
rider like a frivolous panache
of victory. A butterfly
caught stealing colour from the wallpaper
behind her picture as we lift it down
makes use of semaphore to fly away.
Detail sharpens like a change of weather
about the chestnut horse and sick
green deeps of fields and woods. The house
stands back as if in disrepair
or disrepute. A Georgian sash –
left, as we survey it, of the portico –
slides open to invite us to be clever
before the light goes and discover ashes
of a writ cold in a hearth, a bear-skin rug
stained darkly, and a dressing-gown
about the shoulders of a shadow –
in life it seems more cavalier than lucky –
that smiles to see a riding-crop swung high
then takes a razor to remorse
and sends the afterthought of summer, quick
but dying, from the empty room
with little mockeries of lordly shrug
that will not pay the artist or the jockey.

The Vacant Blue

The Hon Gertrude Pringle receives a letter from Lord Blaxter, 1931

Last week was shards of amphorae, the sun
behind you and your shadow on clear water
among the rocks. Today it's blossoms
and fragrances, a bulletin on figs
with ouzo at the harbour in the cool
of evening as your perfect summer passes.
Your wife, the first one of my several mothers –
prescribed green nettle whippings for emotions
of an unseemly sort – speaks well of you
now you've become a cultivated man
and grown into a right and proper person
to write in an ancestral voice
the way a father should, and all such fathers
beside such oceans among mausoleums
and tumbled columns of such ruined cities.
Well. Self-absorption is a vice
Mama of course condones. I have drawn up
your horoscope. It seems to show
instead of signs and planets and transitions
a not-to-be-forgiven vacant blue.
The bung-holes of retsina kegs
you say have pine-branch bungs. Call to that waiter
named after a philosopher. Take supper
among the grey pistachio trees.
Reach for your pad and pen. The boys that crew
the pink-sailed boats politely offer
their pretty sisters in their summer dresses.

The Night Chapel

Although the floor beneath our hooves is pasture
the grass is not enough. We're brought

each evening to this room of darkening air
where cantors lead us with our throats

extended in the bleating prayer
we know instinctively – unlike the goats

who learn their raucous chants by rote –
which begs our ovine gods for human posture

and proper meals of cake and caviar.
Set free at last from scabies and the bloat

we'll ride to town at dawn on Shanks's mare
like upright citizens in woollen coats

to promulgate the cause and flock to vote
for sheep-pens and the abattoir.

Epithalamium

His beard is safe from razor blades. His mind
is firm among the cypresses.

She is the haughtiest of pretty Misses.
The smell of their constraint is like an ache

our darting tongues explore. They must unwind
and lie down in the sun beside us

to share our mattress of embroidered moss
and learn to tolerate our lipless kisses,

our gifts of leaves and twigs, the cake
we'll make for them of mud, our cold caresses.

A Shepherd to His Lass

Beloved, I am speaking from the heart
of artifice. Please do not ask

that sperm shall cleave the egg, or set up thought
tribunals to take me to task

for insincerity when I report
the loveliness in which you bask.

The Fool

Down at the bungalow, the news
gets worse than ever and excitement grows.

They keep a monkey in a narrow cage
on their verandah among clapped-out tools

inherited from me. I look like him.
He has a palliasse and God's fresh breeze

to keep him cool. Van Gogh's straw hat
makes sure his brain stays hot. They gaze

right through him to my favourite sins,
the ones they most abhor there in the dim

light strained through blinded windows
behind which they peel earthworms, spatchcock sparrows,

torture carrots, and perfect the handicrafts
that will sustain them in the coming age

when streams die in their beds and summer shadows –
no longer airborne over woods and meadows –

turn liver-coloured as the poles unfreeze
and AstroTurf warms up by pools

they slither into from hand-woven rafts,
sourced locally, to soothe their papery skins

through which the blue arse of the monkey shows
who meanwhile sings and picks his nose.

Le Pendu

His views – as yours are – were unorthodox.
Air was his element. Because of that
winds blew round him in the calmest weather
and it was in a gust of one he went
to leave us understaffed. His cloak and hat
are here together with his books
and papers by the glimmering pool
among the bulrushes, still wearable.
Try them for size behind that burly spruce,
deracinated, undermined by water,
and half-submerged as if to represent
the mood in which he toiled to raise the veil
of Nature and survey her face.
His own as he grew wise grew terrible
like terracotta with a fiery squint
and he would pounce on all rebukes
to his authority. No rule
of calculation could I think reduce
our line of business to the commonplace
and you would find your colleagues far from dull.
When he became unbearable
they sometimes chose to hang him by the heel,
inverting into smiles his mordant looks,
from that same tree until it fell
and watch the zephyrs comb his dangling locks.

Sentinels

Far sooner than I had supposed
the breathing ocean has begun to creep
about the sharp prehensile toes

of phosphorescent salamanders,
immense and beautiful, who keep
close watch outside the cave where couched on wrack –

like all good parents back to back –
lie those who laughed with me at my own blunders
when time permitted and now sleep.

The Drowned Heads

They lie in ooze beneath the broad meander
of our attention and recall
though quick with water weed – each twin a shock
of verdant hair and beard – the tapping maul,

a chisel warm on their now blurring features.
Sometimes a shadow, as if brushing dust
from these wise marble brows, strews bubbles
in winking wreaths. Their bodies rest

as rubble in adjoining pastures
to keep the landscape calm. They were the first –
because they ponder all our troubles –
to sense that love of mind for stone persists

submerged within our cold romantic natures
and love moreover for unquarried rock
which will in time demand the same surrender
carved form insists on of the block.

The Owl Herb

She who no night bird ever taught
To sing, not what it must, but ought.

WALTER DE LA MARE

I'm in a deep hedge like a child out late
beside the lane. I cup my leaves
around the flower of my beak. My voice insists
through curtained windows, bolted doors,

and soon obedient somnambulists
up from their beds on clicking claws –
the whiskery, the fanged and furred –
pull on their uniforms of human skin

dropped carelessly on bedroom floors
and search for me. Such dreamy lives
produce good meat I hang in skeins
old spiders would call gossamer

to eat at leisure among frosted thistles –
less like a plant, more like a bird
from whom there won't be long to wait
before the true shout of the owl is heard.

Spraunce

The bald rock got in at the beginning,
a mirage so to speak, though not like those
we fell for in the desert, spinning

tanks and trucks from heat waves. I suppose
her cigarette smoke was the haze
that veiled it in the estuary. Her clothes

came off. She made me look. A kid in those days,
a lot too young for grown-up girls
to bother with you'd think. You'd be amazed.

Her tongue and fingers, crimped blonde curls
all over me. Those mewing sounds.
Perhaps that's why I mixed up girls and gulls.

Just over there it happened. On the sands.
I had to help her button up her dress.
She said she'd send her brother round

to belt me if I blabbed. I thought the fuss
she made would get her pregnant and she'd blame me.
The smell of female sweat still makes me queasy.

I didn't understand that she was happy
doing that noise, like crying only sharper.
After school it was the army.

Dodging Rommel. Then the kind of caper –
accounts and such – that's no great shakes but steady.
Computers came and that was time to scarper.

It's strange how many women have been ready
to flash the go-ahead as bold as brass.
And married women. Once a titled lady.

I'd never tell them and they'd never guess
the reason why I fobbed them off.
I think the bald rock saved me, more or less,

from going barmy with the shell-shock stuff,
explosions, guts and beaks, and finger-ends.
Thank God it's calmed down now. I've had enough.

Most summer nights I raise a few tall gins –
here on the front lawn by the patch of pampas –
to all consenting lovers in the dunes

and silt and salt, all seas and rivers.
Although the medics have me down for cancer
it's still the thought of sex that gives me shivers.

I take the treatment, look quite spraunce.
Who knows, maybe reprieve is on the cards.
I'll settle for a 50/50 chance

and the sea view from my bungalow towards
the old bald rock there in his wig of birds.

The Graiae and the Matelot

Morning brings an itch for brisk endeavour.
Their greedy mouths – below each nose
and *inter faeces et urinem* – gape

in expectation but he slips his tether
and grabs his grip and smells the vast
arousal of the sea. He drops his keys

beside his coffee cup. The eye of truth
blinks its finger-lids and slithers
as if down æons between six gnarled knees

to roll through crumbs and orange peel.
The sisters will cry monstrous rape
and breach of promise and spit feathers.

Meanwhile cold coffee dregs congeal
his presence into vacant past
and all their fingertips are eyes skinned-over

that search his absence for their common tooth,
clean knickers, and the mythic rose
he promised when they first shacked up together.

The Star

There is a time for the evening under starlight,
A time for the evening under lamplight
(The evening with the photograph album).

T.S. ELIOT

Like follies – batty monuments to mood –
the trees stay out again all night
their branches rocking nests of dreaming singers.
She sprawls on moon-warmed sky, her long hair spread,
surrounded by eternal picnic food.

It's on her armpits where her dress is damp
and on the moist impression where her tight
belt gripped that recollection lingers
as if the taste of salt might rouse the dead
to close the album and put out the lamp.

The Chrysalis

She had been childless until late one day
when all sides of the house were casting shadow
projected by the sinking sun
or by the rising moon. Only the stone
flags of the terrace glowed, and the chrysalis
that lay there good as gold and loveable,
breathing like blossom in the dark
and half a metre long. She took it in.
Next morning as red insects swarmed
against the windows and a trout
on the cold slab in the pantry rolled its eye
she placed it on the broad lip of the fountain
despite the thin east wind and pointed out
the steeple on the hill among the trees
although of course it could not see.
It slept upon her lap that afternoon
when she had company to hear the priest
discuss the evidence for Noah's Ark
but no one noticed it. It didn't show
itself in that way ever. But it grew
and then transmogrified and flew away,
iridescent and immense, so beautiful
it left her all a-flutter and transformed
back into a child herself, quick as a lark,
on cherub's wings above her vacant pew.

An Evening on the River

An undergraduate of Christmas College
makes a good thrust, gripping sand
at just the right depth, and his punt
turns homeward into darkness with a chuckle.
Animals as if in prayer dream steamily
along the bank – oxen or asses –
and are at peace. But sacrilege
preoccupies the student, and how best
to climb the chapel roof at night
and crown an angel with a chamber pot,
then own up and accept a reprimand
before descending on his family
for festal sweetmeats and the game of Bear.

It seems at first preposterous that Jesus –
on all fours with the beasts – jumps out to stand
alongside on the platform of the water.
Although He is as limned by Holman Hunt,
below His nightshirt there are hooves not feet
and flies are busy in His beard and hair.
His lamp shines starkly on the seat
among the waterproofs and fishing tackle
where a Pre-Raphaelite Madonna sits
but soothes, at her uncovered breast,
no Christ-child. The lithe imp she nurses
belches as it snuffs the light
with one black toe-nail and begins to suckle.

A Slice of Lime

The cotoneaster with its paws of snow
confronts us and is yet another
reason to skulk safely, gin in hand, and gaze.
The doorstep is a pillow. Rest my head
among collapsing buffaloes,
walruses with beaks, accumulations
of dog-skulls in dunces' caps, breasts and boas,
griffins with their stark wings raised
to prop a pall of sky. That world would smother
us all beneath cold teddybears.
A slice of lime tilts forward on my nose.
Our wishes for enfoldment are not dead.
One night we shall wake up and go
to sleep below the dimples and striations
of awful purity. Snow is our mother.

January 2010

New Poems

(2013)

The African Queen

Her comings and her goings were unplanned
and no one minded them. She dashed off screeds
of muddled-up impressions she would pack
inside the cushions and in people's pockets.
Glimpses of encounters with herself in glades
or dreams beneath some wise and whispering tree
were pleasing to her readers on the whole.
They did not like the larger centipedes.
It was a different continent you see.
Her forests in the end became continuous
and led into a once volcanic bowl
then upwards to its molten sunset rim.
When she believed that she had company
she said that she was happy here with us
and never mentioned home or Her or Him.
At last of course the trees ran out of land
and if indeed she left then she came back
unnoticed and ordinarily. One day
she told a tradesman in the corridor
that she met bat-eared foxes in the thickets,
dassies and quick monkeys by a grinding shore
where all that washed up was already sand
but not the whimsical and ruthless creatures
that all her journeys took her looking for.

The Square

A young Lord Blaxter is staying in Islington
with his uncle the Hon Benson Pringle, 1904

The eyes of windows set in jaundiced walls
among the clematis and blowzy roses
peer back half-blinded by the sun.
Gardens with green railings bloom. Hush grows deeper.
I hear ideas begin to flow! Your pen
scrapes busily a room away.
Our modest square holds little more than one
broad mulberry tree, already tall
before the houses came. The day
seems endless in the heat. I'd like to take
that moment when a water-bird – that rises
and recognises stream or lake
by shimmer – banks and smoothly falls
towards it in instinctive joy
and make it mine. I would remain
within it and forget this stifling roost.
The gentleman next door – whose housekeeper
would not suit *me*, I have to say –
is building for himself an apparatus
through which to hear the last thoughts of a brain
obtained from the paupers' hospital.
He has invited you to dine, dear boy!

Vampire Writers

Rats patter keyboards like professionals
in attics. Another century has sped.

A huge glass-fronted gothick cabinet
reflects a window and a shelf

of reliquaries seems absurdly set
in shrubbery with Chinese ivories

together with a likeness of himself
in miniature when he was someone else.

Although perhaps too crude for Hilliard,
pride and sufficiency of pelf

are well portrayed, and zeal in their retention.
Its pallor and the crimson lips disturb.

Shadows slip like shedded dresses down the trees.
Bark is shimmering and autumn foliage thrills

in expectation of his close attention.
A surge of hungry memories

lifts him from dream to appetite
without a jolt and then from bed

to look out and by looking to absorb
the colour from his garden, then the light.

Because their fiction must be fed
the rats will not find darkness untoward.

Augenlicht

The place we've come to leans against the sky
and dreams the moon. A midden steams.
We start a hare. We are alive.

The roads we took were intricate
and bad. Though fearful we were not deterred.
A pale girl gathers shadows from the track.

She whispers an irrevocable word
of which no meaning will survive.
She is inured to working late.

The night is old. Her one bright eye
fades from our way. She's what she seems.
She moves the oceans when she turns her back.

Comb Hill

Polite attention at the very least
is due to what this is that darts and whirrs
against the solid daylight of the window.
I pay it. I pull out a book
on demonology and hope to learn
its name and attributes. It bares its face.

Which is absurd. Trees turn to look
expectantly three fields away. The wind
breathes softly but begins to blow
more briskly as my mind cuts loose to race
down corridors of conifers
on wing-blur in a crush of air and sound.

The wood is soon a bristling pelt, a beast
within it, snorting. It is gaining ground.
When eyes were compound and when speech was verse
our books were stones. Here's one to throw.
Light shatters and the trees return
to looking inward at a darker place.

Future Perfect

Go out to where the garden was and stand
in my mind's eye out of sight and smell the rain.
Now press the damp earth with your thumb
so gently as to be all but unfelt.
In the modern paradise each heart's desire
is met. We loll in dentists' chairs. We're fed
by athletes at an operating table.
All is exactly as we hoped and planned.
Reflect on that until your mind is numb.

Then think of gardening. Do not aspire
as we once did to make your life resemble
let's say the cantilever of a crane
or else the vast curve of a concrete vault
beneath which robots march. Ignore the fault
that opens underneath each dock or bramble.
Search for the last trace of the shed
where clean tools are stacked ready for the hand.
Start digging when the ground begins to melt.

Mademoiselle de Silhouette

As she stepped outside she heard the furniture
begin to move. She left the door ajar
in case it wished to follow her
to this small café open to the air
where there might just be room beneath the awning
behind the fence of privet bushes
for chair and table and her knick-knack shelf,
her looking-glass and scissor drawer.
The *trottoir* dapples in the sun.
A tree is pinkly pearl in bloom and thrushes
dart and chirrup their intention
to keep on simulating fun. *Voilà*.
For one bright day her darkest self
has snipped away its context. She is yawning.

Uncle Benson

> *His dead body lay constantly on its face on the bier,*
> *although it had been five times turned upwards.*
>
> JOHANN GAST, *Sermones Conviviales*

He wouldn't read and so we didn't write
mais au fil du temps we found a few things out.
He had become a nuisance to the place.
There was a long chair on the lawn
in half-light under stars. All he required
was an autonomous existence on it
at all times of the day or night.
His dream feet took him there repeatedly.
He found a voice unlike his own,
dredged up somehow from within, in which he'd shout
and leave no doubt where he desired
to get to. Expeditiously.
Staff turned him conscientiously and yet
like Faust they always found him on his face.
He'd nothing else to do day after day
but scribble stuff about some gloomy pasture
with dusty hedges and a slope
that led up to a nebulous horizon
where Shining Forms were following the sun
as it went down and him there, bodiless
apparently, yet able to draw breath
enough to help them warble out a number
he called the Music of the Spheres.
It was his hobbyhorse. It helped him cope.
But there were voices asking him to stay
and that suggested cerebral imposture.
Or so the doctor said, and took his fee.
He had a childhood he would not remember
yet sensed a refuge and a hope

beyond this world of echo and penumbra
and wished to tell us so. His fear
was not, he'd say, of mockery
but that we'd never see what he had seen.
He kept the nonsense going until death
caught sight of him and visions seemed less fun
than raving about furniture.
Since no one cares to read tomfoolery
we thought it best to place his limp *cahier*
with due respect upon the fire
to blaze up and die down and rise away.

Paris 1929

Curiosity in Bolam Woods

Dead leaves are whispering by the lough
and how ethereal reaching boughs
appear despite their massiveness. The moon

observed me closely as she rose.
The one that walks here will be soon.
I hear the scrape of his sharp toes

on frozen ground. I hear his cough.
If I see him I shall do my best to laugh.
He wears my face with its long nose.

Venus Among the Ruins

I wait for you in no time but your own.
Where my blank eyes appear to glance
sections of a column sink like room-sized cogs
where they were toppled. My hand and head
reveal the love the sculptor had
for fine stone and my countenance.
These are my last remains, unknown
to archaeologists and pedagogues.
Camp fires smoulder. There is jigging
to thwacking music and a choir of dogs.
I hold a marble telephone
and listen to a pythoness unpicking
autobiographical significance.
She divines that in the long run we are dead.

The Mistress

She smiles with mild approval at the world
of which she is the hub. Her shrubberies
and pampas clumps in cared-for air
conceal our loyal faces. It's the hour
when voices carry but there is no word.
She feels no duty to acknowledge us
but remains in the mind's eye motionless
and never changing. Part of a veranda
behind her is in focus and a gable
tipped by a spike yet she is blurred.
The day is overcast. The camera
snaps up the glare of her pale dress.
We're snobs and therefore seldom envious.
The treasure box in which her future curled
at birth is ours though we've become unable
to bring ourselves to think of that. Alas
whereas we hardly recognise each other
she understands exactly who she is.

The Podiatrists

On stage we'd have a row of chairs and sprawl
barefoot and stretch our legs. There would be cheers.
We'd give 'em *Sparse Northern Woods* – our act was noise –
then cap that with the sound that ends the dream
we all had then of burial.
At every pause we'd grin like naughty boys
immaculate in evening dress and drum
our heels until our pink feet bounced
to more applause. Oh yes. When we announced
The Last Chime of a Bell Obscurely Shed
by a Foxglove in a Long Lost Autumn
they'd pelt us with blown kisses. The years. The years.
The crowds that queued all day to hear us fled.
Shoes clove to us. Our toes went dumb.

The Suitor

She's in a deckchair with a magazine
it is too dark to read. A foal unsteady
in the shelter of its mother dances
between timidity and jubilance.
Its whinny from two fields away
reaches the faintly gleaming page.
The sky blew clear but now the breeze is gentle.
Last evening his fatuity
betrayed itself. Back came the flashing glance,
the trilling tone, the grandiosity
of gesture. Her soul advances
towards its youth with confidence
but she is conscious of her age.
The constellations open and remain.
She never used to be so temperamental.
Her taxi is still standing in the lane.

Eden Lodge

By bedtime they'd seen little of the place
beyond the lobby and the bridal suite
but juggled their impressions as they slept.
Next day they put these to the test and found
the room they occupied had steps
down to a garden. Naked when they rose
they strolled the lawn and had no thought of hiding.
Their shadows reached an apple tree.

The branches moved. They saw your face
and knew that they were loved. There was no doubt.
I helped them understand how such love goes
then curled myself to watch them both deciding
to leave before breakfast but then hang about
and slip back when there's nobody around –
particularly you and me –
to eat your fruit and dress then hit the street.

The Fancier

The shower door opens in an arc of drip.
When she parts the bedroom curtains there is light
enough to see the cosy traps
and cages where she keeps the singing
that once delighted her. It's time to write
the last note in her diary of care
for unwise birds. She'll add a sketch
of one that spoiled it all for her this morning
by speaking. She draws it quick and green and small.

They'll have to go. So must she. Larks will fall.
Crows on the road will cark a warning
then peck her shadow and drop dead. Last night
she failed to crank up the contraption
that fills her nest with warmth and glare
and helps to soothe the cruel itch
that prompts the birdseed and the scattered scraps
and kindnesses that are beyond description.
She chirrups as she curls her lip.

Summer on Fourlaws Fell

It's getting late and yet we daren't be quick.
The day grows crystalline then dim. The trees

are amplifying shadow. Let's begin
to grasp the afternoon. We'll make a rule

that sheep stop feeding as we pass.
Scuts of rabbits vanish. A suggestion

of snake will slip from path to heather
while unkind insects chuckle in the grass.

We are not fools. It's quite the contrary.
Our wisdom though exceeds what we remember.

Let's say this hazy sunshine has an eye
for butterflies. The air is thick

with indecision. Lazy bees
consort with redolence. We'll teach each other

what's hard to know. Time is our school.
The year is once again almost September.

NOTES

The Long Pack (21-39)

The story of the long pack appears in *The Ettrick Shepherd's Tales*, and also in Elizabeth Gaskell's *Cranford*. It is well known in the village of Bellingham, in Northumberland, where the occupant of the pack is buried in the churchyard. My poem adds details of his earlier life, as a member of a community of Ranters, to material provided by James Hogg, together with an account of some episodes in the lives of two late-twentieth-century lovers who are troubled by this desperado's restless and rather domineering spirit. The haunter's aim is to be reborn and recognised. Meanwhile he describes their experiences as well as his own, offers advice and comment, and appears sometimes in foliage, like the Green Man. The narrator also refers, perhaps unwisely, to links between participants in the 1715 Jacobite uprising in Northumberland and the activities of the mysterious Prieuré de Sion, described by Michael Baigent, Richard Leigh, and Henry Lincoln in *The Holy Blood and the Holy Grail*. The voice of Richard Last, which dominates the chorus, is adapted from the writings of the real-life Ranter Abiezer Coppe. The chorus also includes quotations from Sir George Etherege, Robert Herrick, Samuel Johnson, Andrew Marvell, the anonymous author of 'Hexham Wood', and Wilfrid Gibson, whose poem 'The Unseen Rider' also mentions Heatherbell and the tragic wedding. Apart from a visit to the Coromandel coast, and to the unusual church at Hartburn, the events of the poem all take place in the North Tyne valley and Redesdale. The ruins of The Orchard can still be visited.

Jigger Nods (65-86)

Iphicles was the son of Amphitrion and his wife Alcmene, but his brother Hercules was the son of Zeus, who had disguised himself as Amphitrion. The relationship of Henry Jigger to his brother, the popular GP, corresponds to that between Hercules and Iphicles, though in this case Zeus had disguised himself as the vicar. As a schoolmaster, somewhere in the northern part of England in the middle of the last century, Jigger likes to dwell, in a muddled sort of way, on the story of the occupation of Albion by the Trojan

Brutus, in which Hercules played a part. There is of course no excuse for his disreputable views, moral cowardice and heavy drinking, or for his addiction to Latin tags. Quotations throughout the poem are taken or adapted from *Albion's England* by William Warner, of which C.S. Lewis wrote: 'The good things are as far divided as the suns in space.' The Latin tags may be found underlined in the section headed 'Words and Phrases in More or Less Current Use from Latin, Greek, and Modern Foreign Languages' in Jigger's copy of *Chambers's Twentieth Century Dictionary*, 1939 edition, and, for convenience, below. The exception, *Non Nisi Malis Terrori*, remains the motto of the school that employed him.

Jigger's Latin tags: Aut insanit homo aut versus facit (either the man is mad or making verses); Bis pueri senes (old men are twice boys); Claviger (club-bearer or key-bearer, an epithet of Hercules); Dum vivimus vivamus (while we live, let us live); Eheu fugaces… labuntur anni (alas, the fleeting years slip away); Ex pede Herculem (we recognise Hercules by his foot); Fuimus Troes (we were once Trojans); Necessitas non habet legem (necessity has or knows no law); Obscurum per obscurius (explaining the obscure by means of the more obscure); O zonam perdidit (he has lost his purse, he is in needy circumstances).

Folly Wood (107-18)

George Ripley, who died in 1490, was an important English alchemist. The subtitles of the thirteen sections of the poem are the names of the Twelve Gates, or stages in the alchemical process, as set out in his *Compound of Alchymy*, plus the recapitulation. They are of course in a different order.

Gustav Mahler Returns to Maiernigg (138)

Mahler is associated with the character of the writer Gustav von Aschenbach in Thomas Mann's *Death in Venice*. In Luchino Visconti's film version he is played by Dirk Bogarde, who resembled Mahler, and recast as a composer whose work is derided. 'Caterpillars crawl' is from Andrew Marvell.

Unity in the Englischer Garten (139)

Unity Valkyrie Mitford, who liked to call the Nazi stormtroopers 'dear storms', was brought up at Swinbrook in Oxfordshire. She shot herself in the Englischer Garten in Munich in September 1939, shortly after her twenty-fifth birthday. She survived to die in Scotland in 1948.

Bobby Bendick's Ride (147-54)

The Reverend Robert Bendick and the ballad 'Bobby Bendick's Ride', together with other members of the curious and unlucky Bendick family, are mentioned in a story by Sean O'Brien. The ballad is otherwise hitherto unknown. I like to think I heard it twenty or thirty years ago in the Gun Inn in Ridsdale, on the evening of Bellingham Show, but that is impossible, because I wrote it. It appears that Bendick studied in France rather than at Oxford or Cambridge, perhaps to save money or to distance himself from scandal. What is known about his family would suggest the latter. His ordination would have taken place during the time of the Commonwealth, though no record of it has been found, and though his activities at and around the Norman church of St Cuthbert at Corsenside cannot be dated with certainty they clearly took place during the long reign of the 'sordid and scandalous' John Graham, who was the curate there from 1617 to 1682, and, we must assume, with his connivance. Bendick was evidently familiar with Pau and the neighbouring town of Lescar, where the mosaic of the crippled huntsman can be seen in the church of Notre-Dame beside the tombs of some of the kings of Navarre. The Musée des Beaux Arts in Pau houses more paintings on the theme of Tobias and the Angel – alias Azariah – than a visitor might expect, no doubt reflecting the interests of a former benefactor. The city is also proud to be the birthplace of Henry IV of France, whose cradle was a turtle shell, and of Jean-Baptiste Bernadotte, the 'sergeant with beautiful legs', who became King of Sweden. A later member of the English colony in Pau was Major C.W. Mercer, who wrote as Dornford Yates. The genial voice of his creation Bertram 'Berry'

Pleydell echoes here and there in the poem. I am indebted to an article by Helen Grant, published in *The Ghosts and Scholars M.R. James Newsletter*, for the information that nine crocodiles are dedicated ancient monuments in France. According to J.C. Cooper and other authorities, the crocodile symbolises duplicity and viciousness but is also considered to be a guardian of knowledge. The jaws of the crocodile represent hell. Wanney Byre is a fissure in the face of Great Wanney Crag. 'Cuddy's kirk' has been repaired since Bendick's time, and is used for occasional services. I have been unable to corroborate a report that children in that secretive corner of Northumberland used to be warned to stay away from Ingram Pool after dark for fear of meeting 'Black Bobby'. There are after all less fanciful reasons to avoid deep water at night.

The Graiae and the Matelot (168)

The Graiae were Pemphredo, Enyo, and Deino, monstrous sisters and protectors of the Gorgons. They had one eye and one tooth between them. *'Inter faeces et urinem nascimur'* (we are born between faeces and urine) is from St Augustine.

Peter Bennet was born in Leek, Staffordshire, in 1942. He went as a scholarship boy to King's School Macclesfield, and then to Manchester College of Art and Design, where he was influenced by the painter Norman Adams and his wife, the poet Anna Adams. He taught in secondary and further education, including two years' work with redundant men following the closure of Consett Steel Works, and subsequently spent sixteen years as Tutor Organiser for Northumberland with the Workers' Educational Association. He gave up painting for writing in 1980 and did a part-time MA in Modern English and American Literature at Newcastle University, including a study of W.S. Graham.

He has received major awards from New Writing North and Arts Council England and been a prizewinner in the National and the Arvon International Poetry Competitions, and in the Basil Bunting Awards. His books include *Sky-Riding* (1984) from Peterloo Poets; *All the Real* (1994), *Goblin Lawn: New and Selected Poems* (2005), *The Glass Swarm* (2008) and *The Game of Bear* (2011), from Flambard Press; and *Border* (2013) from Bloodaxe Books. *The Glass Swarm* was a Poetry Book Society Choice in 2008, and was shortlisted for the T.S. Eliot Prize.

He lived for thirty-three years near the Wild Hills o'Wanney in Northumberland, in a remote cottage associated with the ballad writer James Armstrong, author of *Wannie Blossoms*. He now lives in Whitley Bay.